Two Dogs and a Suitcase
Clueless in Charente

Sarah Jane Butfield

Copyright © 2012 Sarah jane Butfield
All rights reserved.

Cover design: Tabatha Designs

Photography by Nigel Butfield

First edition 2014

The people and events in this book are portrayed as perceived and experienced by Sarah Jane Butfield. Some names have been changed for privacy reasons.

The moral right of the author has been asserted.

No part of this book may be reproduced, stored in a retrieval system or transmitted without written permission of the publisher.

ISBN: 1499788622
ISBN-13: 978-1499788624

DEDICATION

To my supportive and patient husband Nigel, who believes in me and everything I do. He enables me to fulfil my passion for writing. I love you, Mr Butfield.

Our mantras

Never give up on your dreams;
if you can conceive it then you can achieve it.

Be yourself. Those who mind do not matter,
those who matter do not mind.

These mantras are always in my heart and they are the mantras by which I now live my life. I keep these particular ones written in my journals, on my desk and in my kitchen.

CONTENTS

Dedication
Acknowledgements
Prologue
1. First impressions
2. Starting over
3. La Grande Tomate
4. Is she ok to be left there alone?
5. The tea towel bandit strikes as renovations begin
6. A boomerang named Jaime
7. Surviving France
8. My garden and other animals
9. Friends, neighbours and other people
10. Frugally does it
11. Hobart to Le Havre
12. Christmas in France
13. Desperate measures
14. Playing at being a tourist
15. Family life changing lanes
16. When all you want is someone to say "Yes"
17. Family time, Felixstowe and an angry rabbit
18. Mothers and daughters
19. An Indie author's dream a reality
20. Gypsy, dreamer or both?

About the author
Books by Sarah Jane Butfield

Epilogue

Professional acknowledgements

Contact Sarah Jane Butfield on these author links

ACKNOWLEDGMENTS

As always, my children support my endeavours in the form of sharing book news and events on social media and promoting sales of my first book, 'Glass Half Full: Our Australian Adventure' to friends and work colleagues. As they do it for no commission, I am thankful and appreciative. To Samantha, Robert, Clair and Jaime especially, a very big thank you.
To my father in law John Butfield, who helps with spreading the word about my books in Australia. He has also put together photographs of my book, 'Glass Half Full: Our Australian Adventure' being read in random places around Australia, including the Royal Hobart Hospital. Thank you also to Cam Williams, my son in law to be, for doing as Samantha tells him, in relation to sharing my social media links.
To Steve Murray and Nigel Butfield, my beta reader team leaders, I could not have done this without you, so thank you. Finally thank you to Tabatha Stirling for her patience and precision with the book cover. It looks amazing.
I would like to extend my gratitude to some of our friends that you will get to know, who became a big part of our story.
Nicky and Tim Day: Without Tim offering Nigel work, and both of them offering their friendship, who knows how long our French experience would have lasted?
Julia and Phil James: Apart from their friendship, they helped us on many practical levels, including the loan of their gas cooker, trees to fell for firewood and in the early days, use of the internet and the bath.
Darren Pitts, our English estate agent in France. Without Darren's help, we would not have found our renovation property or completed on the sale with relative ease. He went beyond the call of duty to help us navigate the French conveyancing process while we were living overseas.

PROLOGUE

It is September, and we are now in the Charente, South West France. Who could have imagined that we would find ourselves moving from the UK to Australia in 2008, only to then move to France in 2012? I believe that there is always something positive to come from any negative situation or experience. However, in 2010, an unexpected negative influence on my life presented itself in the form of a road-rage car accident. I struggled for a long time to find a positive from that event. The accident resulted in my driving anxiety and a diagnosis of post-traumatic stress disorder. The investigations and treatments during the lengthy medical process tested my psychological strength in a variety of ways.

Two years after the accident and with a lengthy legal process now complete, the financial compensation sits in our bank account. The money, and whatever we choose to do with it, will never give me back my independence, in the form of my driving confidence. Does any amount of money reflect an acceptable level of recompense for the lifelong baggage that I carry after the events of that fateful day in April 2010? We decide, after discussing it at length, to use the money to fulfil another of our long held dreams, that of renovating a small cottage in France. To achieve our dream of owning a family home again, after losing our home and the roots to our Australian dream during the Brisbane floods of 2011 is what motivates us.

The process of finding our new home in France, meeting our meagre criteria, brings back memories of excitement, dream chasing and a sense of doing the right thing. When we decide that our desired location is France, we research and identify the best areas for renovation properties at reasonable prices, which are also within easy access to transport links to the UK. The next essential criterion is budget. The exchange rate at the time is favourable for transferring money from Australian dollars to Euros, so our budget for the property purchase and associated fees becomes 25,000 euros. Now for that money you do not end up owning a chateau, or anything resembling a 'normal' home by UK or Australian standards. However what you do get is a base, a family home that we will fill with love, laughter and unconditional support.

Our initial search area on the internet is around Montmorillon. This riverside town, situated in the Vienne Department of the Poitou Charentes region, has two airports to the North West. Poitiers airport is 50 km away and Limoges airport is 70 km. This allows easy access to cheap Ryanair flights to the UK. It also sits on the main TER (Transport Express Règional) rail link, for easy access to the major cities. The appeal of Montmorillon, with its culture and history, feeds my romantic fantasies of being a successful author living in France. Montmorillon is known as, 'the city of writing,' and this piece of history reinforces my belief that this is the perfect place for me to go and start my writing career. Its medieval charm is captured in the cobbled streets that wind their way through the old quarter. They deliver visitors to an array of chapels, churches and buildings, all oozing with history. The view of the River Gartempe, which flows through this riverside town, is breath taking and to buy a house in Montmorillon is not within our budget. However, there are quite a few renovation property opportunities within a few kilometres' radius. Our internet search identifies ten potential properties in the villages of La Trimouille, Magnac Laval and Gencay. The lengthy logistical timeframe that is required for pet vaccinations, my language course and for Jaime to finish school prior to making an international move means we have time to build in a short trip. We need to find a property, start the purchase process and then hope that we can complete on the sale before we arrive permanently, whenever that may be.

A short trip from Australia to France is a contradiction in terms, but with the permission of the bankruptcy trustees, given the rationale for our move, we are free to go. We stay at Les Chambres de la Loge, a small chambre d'hote, or bed and breakfast, just outside Montmorillon, run by a French couple, Nathalie Patrier and Daniel Capillon. Nathalie speaks English as she has travelled in the UK, and she is keen to learn new words and phrases. Together they have tastefully restored the old house to establish three comfortable guest rooms, each named after local features and all with en-suite, television, Wi-Fi, welcome tray on arrival and a private entrance. Ours is the Gartempe room. Nathalie serves an exquisite French breakfast with homemade bread, jams and croissants in a beautiful dining room or, on sunny mornings, on the terrace. At breakfast on the first morning, Nathalie serves the coffee and makes conversation with us in English. A second couple joins us at the table and start a conversation in French with Nathalie. Although they occasionally glance at us, we cannot understand or engage in the conversation so we just chat quietly between ourselves. Nathalie, obviously feeling a bit uncomfortable that we are not able to participate, diverts the conversation a couple of times. She asks a question in English as if she is going to translate our reply for the other couple. Nigel is more concerned that despite how much the man has to say he is eating all the croissants!

It is nice for us and the other guests that we do not have to come through the main house, especially as we are in and out a lot during the viewings over the next few days. We can go to the garden, which has a bistro table and chairs, to enjoy a glass of wine as we peruse property details. We hire a car and arrive with a short list of ten properties lined up for viewing.

Day one of our five day stay; Darren, the estate agent, calls to say only two of the ten properties shortlisted are still for sale. He suggests that we extend our search area given our limited time in France for viewings. We view the two remaining properties from our shortlist with disappointment. Not disappointment at the properties themselves, or even the remote locations, but the fact that the gardens are not near to the properties. We now know this is a French consequence of inheritance laws. Sometimes when properties are left in wills to various family members, they sell the barns and gardens, etc., as separate pieces of real estate. The gardens at property number two are across the road, which is too dangerous for our dogs, Dave and Buster. An air of despondency looms as we start to view the details of properties in the Confolens area. Although we have a small budget, we know that we can afford to stipulate a few essential criteria. It must have walls, connection to utilities and the roof must be intact.

By the third day of our weeklong viewing trip, we are no nearer to finding a property. We have three properties left to view for our final assault on this mission. It rains heavily on the day we meet Darren to view the final properties. As we pull up and park across the road from the first house, from the outside, it does not say 'buy me.' However, there is something about it, which charms and fascinates me. I sense a spiritual connection, which sounds bizarre I know, as I have never been to, or even heard of, this little village before. Maybe it has something to do with the proximity of the village church that overlooks the road to this bland little cottage.

"Now, how flexible are you prepared to be on the condition of the roof?" Darren says.

As Nigel firmly grips my hand I realise that we are both thinking the same thing, we cannot afford to make a reactive, desperation purchase. If we are going to consider a compromise, there needed to be other redeeming features to compensate.

"What do you mean by flexible?" Nigel asks.

"Well the roof of the house is intact, but there is damage to the roof in the barn," he says.

"Ok, well that's not so bad, I suppose, let's go take a look."

I am a bit uneasy about this, as we are not experienced renovators.

As Darren struggles to unlock the front door with a long thin key, the rain drips down my neck from the leaking guttering. The daylight from the open door shows us the way as we walk straight through the house. I say house, but it resembles an animal shelter; the floor is unmade and sloping, pieces of wood and bags of what I assume are belongings are piled in the corners. We reach the back door that leads into the garden.

Here is my redeeming feature. The garden is perfect. Currently resembling a meadow, with a babbling brook on the boundary, it looks out onto nothing except fields and trees all the way to the horizon. Standing in the rain, I turn and look back at the house and adjacent barn, and the true enormity of the degree of flexibility we need to exercise in relation to the roof hits me. There is a hole, where a large piece has caved in, which lets the rain into the barn. The barn is not accessible from the back garden, as the doorway is overgrown with what appear to be bushes and weeds. It is raining too hard to investigate further. We go back inside and head upstairs to explore the living area. This area has plastic sheeting under leaks in the ceiling and old wine bottles in the corner of the front bedroom. It is like a scene from a scary movie like, 'Hostel,' with its stained walls, hanging garments of clothing and the appearance of damp. Darren opens the shutters and immediately, despite it being a grey day outside, the potential shines in revealing oak floors and beams. I do not know why, because it is not what I envisaged us buying, but I think I love it.

We finish looking around the house and enter the barn from the front. Inside it is full of rubbish, straw and roof debris. Everything is wet and green with moss and mould. Can this ever be made into anything resembling a house?

We drive on to the other properties. One has pink walls throughout, which I can deal with, but it has broken glass from what appears to be a break-in. Immediately this says, 'no way' to me, especially in such a remote location. The next has no garden of any useful size. I think my mind is still at the first property that we viewed today. We head back to Montmorillon discussing and debating our options. I have made up my mind; I want that house regardless of the roof damage. We review our budget and decide that we will put in a cheeky offer, which will give us 10,000 euros for a roof repair, surely that will be enough? I call Darren and he puts in the offer. An anxious overnight wait leads to acceptance of our offer the following morning. Excited at finding our renovation project and new home, we arrange to go for a second viewing, on our own, to take photographs to help us plan our renovation work schedule and to get quotes for the roof repair. The music to accompany our French property-buying trip has been the new Lana Del Rey album, 'Born to Die,' which Nigel brought with him. It is the only music CD we have with us. The French radio channels do not make easy listening when you cannot understand the language. We listen to the album on repeat so the words to 'Summertime Sadness' and 'Video Games' come to mind whenever I recall our buying trip.

Sometimes I wonder if we could or would have achieved this dream from our personal bucket list, had it not been for the floods and the car accident, who knows? We now own a home, albeit uninhabitable by some less resilient people's standards. With no mortgage, we are confident that no person or act of Mother Nature will ever take it away from us. One thing that I do know is that from the moment we arrived here our lives changed, both on a physical and psychological level. Life is good.

CHAPTER 1 FIRST IMPRESSIONS

Notre nouvelle maison (Our new home)

"Open the door, key man!"

As keys never seem to operate properly in my hands, the term key man has become one of our in-house jokes. Either that or I lose or sometimes even break them. Therefore, over the last sixteen years, Nigel has always been my key man. He takes charge of opening and locking up wherever we go, whether it is at home, on holiday or at work. I often wonder how I survived so many years of nursing carrying a bunch of keys in my pockets. Keys to drugs cupboards, treatment and storerooms never gave me any problems, it is only ever with my personal keys.

"Have some patience will you; you're worse than the kids when you get excited."

The key does not appear to fit. It is raining hard and our Australian cattle dogs, our precious boys, Dave and Buster, are barking loudly in their sky crates in the back of the hire-car. Just as they have for the whole of the five-hour journey from Paris. Nigel is quick to work out that the lock mechanism is upside down. Therefore, the key needs to go in upside down and so he needs to turn the key in an anti-clockwise direction, instead of clockwise, in our quirky French door. The word door does not give an accurate description of the entrance to our new home. It resembles the entrance to a grotto or an animal shelter, with its rusty wrought iron latch. There is a metal grid over a small frosted glass windowpane, crudely fitted into the grey painted wood door. A large oak lintel above the doorway is partly obscured by peeling render. The wood peeps out, tempting us with the potential splendour ahead. We are keen to begin unveiling the hidden charm and features of our two hundred year old cottage.

In true French style, the door opens into 'la cave,' meaning cellar, or lower part of the house. This area would have been the living quarters for the animals belonging to the household years ago. It was common for each house to have its own goat, cow or sheep for milk and chickens for eggs and meat. For now, our cave is a dumping ground for pieces of wood, bricks and random torn pieces of cloth. They hang on large nails from the walls, for reasons unknown for now. The living area, again a term I use in loose and not literal way, is on the first floor.

Inside, darkness prevails. As our eyes strain to adjust and refocus, the stench of long standing dampness seeps into my nostrils. This smell takes my mind back to when the children were at school. That smell of mouldy bread crusts, in Rob's overlooked lunchbox at the end of the weekend, evokes the Proust Phenomenon. Proust folk law says that odours are especially powerful reminders of autobiographical experiences, taking you immediately back to the exact place and time. So it was with the aroma inside the house.

The door immediately to our left leads to the staircase. However, it yields a hand written message, on yellow stained paper, in bold black letters. It is in French written exactly as it below. Despite the language barrier, the use of large bold, capital letters makes it obvious that it denotes a warning of some description.

ATTENTION L'ELECTRICITE EST COUPEE ET LES BOITE A FUSIBLE EST DERRIERE VOUS!!

Our eyes meet in subliminal acknowledgement of our amateurish approach to this adventure. We are unable to read or understand the French sign in front of us. Not for the first time the French to English dictionary comes in handy as eventually we discover the meaning of the message.

WARNING ELECTRICITY IS CUT AND FUSE BOX IS BEHIND YOU!!

I find the exclamation marks alarming. Does it mean watch out, beware or take heed? We look at the box and then at each other. The house has been empty for several years since the owner went into an aged care facility. With that in mind, dare we push the switch to allow electricity to flow through the ancient wiring of our new home? We know we have no choice, it is five o'clock on a rainy day in September and already the daylight is fading. Nigel gingerly switches it on with a piece of wood at arm's length and steps back, his eyes squinting in trepidation. We hold our breath, in anticipation of light or some sign that the electricity is flowing. We groan, as nothing appears to happen. Nigel decides to search the walls for a light switch. As he moves towards the staircase, he notices a sliver of light coming from under the misshapen door. It appears that the only light bulb in the house is upstairs. It is hanging from what resembles twisted, brown, unravelling wool above the staircase.

The oak staircase displays the visual evidence of many years usage. The well-trodden stair-treads slant in the centre where footsteps have worn them over the years. Three of the stair-treads reveal evidence of a crude attempt at repair. The addition of pieces of wood nailed on top makes them even more unsafe. The dark brown painted balustrade illuminates with yellow woodworm holes and dust. The handrail shines with the grease of hands grasping it over the years. I follow Nigel up the stairs trying not to touch the handrail, but I am fearful of the stairs' sturdiness, so I hold on tight. For no real reason, I hold my breath as I tread with caution up the stairs. We arrive in the living area, which has a window to the front of the property, with its shutters closed. Opening the window and shutters lets in the remaining light of this dull day. It reveals an array of cobwebs hanging from the oak beams. On the floor, there is a random selection of plastic bags trying without success to protect the floor from the leaking roof.

Two rooms lead off from this living area; the first faces the road to the front, and the other faces the garden at the back. The room at the back has no shutters, and the window reveals the first glimpse of our new garden. Well, at the moment it is more like a piece of wild meadow, with long grass and an array of blackberry bushes leading to the brook that, lined with trees, runs along the boundary of our land. Did we really buy a property with a brook in the garden near to my beloved house, after our Australian flood experience? Yes, is the answer. Our rationale is simple; the brook is typical French rustic style. As usual, we have let our emotions rule our heads with the romanticism of owning our renovation property in rural France. A long held bucket list item now has a big tick against it.

We get the boys from the car and bring in our bags; standing in the cave, we look at each other. Two dogs and a suitcase, this unlikely combination is the entirety of our belongings as we start this new chapter in our lives. Taking the boys into the garden to stretch their legs, we are quick to realise that it is not safe to tie them up outside yet. At least not until we have investigated the ground a bit further. There are pieces of broken pottery, a dilapidated outhouse and the remains of a porcelain toilet. Scattered, they form an unruly mosaic like image, lying on the untouched earth. After looking around, we begin settling the boys in the cave area. Oblivious of time, the sound of church bells ringing pricks at our ears. Nigel looks at his watch; it is seven o'clock in the evening.

"Oh that's lovely; the church clock chimes on the hour."

As we look at each other, Nigel smiles, in that way he does when he is thinking, 'Here she goes again.' In our excitement, neither of us could recall hearing the bells chime on the hour before now. As they continue to chime, more than seven times and in an irregular pattern, we begin to wonder what the significance is. However, there is no time for that now, we need to organise ourselves for the night ahead.

The first night in our new home is a basic affair. In our minimal luggage, we brought two sleeping bags, one inflatable double air mattress and one pillow. We started out with two pillows, but we accidently left Nigel's at the airport hotel in Paris as jet lag consumed us. There is no foot pump for the air mattress. Although it came folded in a neat square to fit in my bag, it took up a large amount of my luggage weight allowance and so we had to relegate the pump to the low priority pile. We are already tired from our five-hour drive today from just outside Paris, yet we take turns blowing air into the mattress, only handing over to one another whenever we are too light headed to continue. Typical of our survival management style, our mantra is 'just get on with it' regardless of the consequences.

Bedtime beckons to us earlier than normal today, after eating our motorway service station sandwiches, which as luck would have it we bought earlier, on our way here. Lucky indeed, because there is no shop nearby, and exhaustion means driving to find one is not a safe or an inviting prospect. As usual, I liken myself to a book character; it is not the tiredness causing this fantasy like behaviour. I do believe I must have the words of a hundred books running through my veins. As my imagination runs-riot, I could be a member of Enid Blyton's, The Famous Five, embarking on an adventure. As we wash down the sandwiches, drinking from a family sized bottle of iced tea, the intensity of our excitement becomes a surreal realisation of our new surroundings. Unsurprisingly, we are unprepared for the environment in which we now expect to be able to live. However, our love of camping means this will be fun, and if I say it enough times, I can make myself believe this.

Well, for Nigel, any thoughts of fun depart as he realises we have to share a pillow, or he will have to use his flight neck support for his head. Our sleepy boys, Dave and Buster, join us on the air mattress for comfort. They have spent far too much time in the sky crates, and they do give us some much-needed warmth. The empty house is stony cold. It resembles the hospital mortuary I used to escort corpses to at St Mary's Hospital during my junior nursing days. With that memory haunting me my imagination goes into overdrive. Has anyone ever died in here? It must be over two hundred years old!

Within minutes, exhaustion consumes me, and I am asleep. In a few hours, our air mattress is flat, and we are all lying on the cold, hard, oak floorboards. Too tired to investigate we remain that way tossing and turning to relieve the pressure of our bodies on our hips. In the darkness, during one particular turn, we realise we are both awake.

"We will laugh about this one day," I say in my cheeky tone that Nigel normally finds funny. He is not laughing now at my attempts to make light of our predicament. He struggles with his neck support, manhandles Dave from across his chest and tries to find a comfortable sleeping position.

We closed the shutters to keep any heat we generate from our bodies overnight in the room. The church bells ringing rudely interrupts my slumber, they sound so loud, as if I am in the bell tower. Do they appear to ring louder when they wake you from a deep sleep? For a split second, I have no idea where I am, and panic encapsulates my mind. Have I been kidnapped? Am I being held for ransom, lying on the floor in a darkened room? I feel across the air mattress for Nigel and the boys; I cannot feel any of them and my initial panic turns to fear. Suddenly the shutters open, sunlight streams in and I see the silhouette of Nigel standing there in front of the window. In a gush of words rambling from my mouth like the proverbial verbal diarrhoea, I explain my initial panic. Nigel just looks at me in that way that he does when I have said or done something 'blonde' as he calls it. I know his tolerance of my vivid imagination and storytelling deserts him when he is concentrating on protecting me and being a caveman. He is my hero. It is a rainy day, and our roof is leaking badly. On a practical level, there is an urgent need for buckets. On a personal level, I have an urgent need of coffee or caffeine in some description. It has been more than sixteen hours since my last coffee, and when my caffeine levels are low it shows. Time to shop, eat and drink coffee but not necessarily in that order.

CHAPTER 2 STARTING OVER

Two knives and forks, but no spoons!

In dire need of caffeine, we decide to head out for coffee and breakfast. We also need some basic shopping for household essentials and food. After a short walk with the boys to the village green, we decide that we cannot leave them home alone, in the cave. With no natural light, we feel sorry for them, and we load them into the sky crates. They are the working dog's version of pampered pooches. The boys could have stayed at home because when we go out they curl up in their crates and sleep the entire time. Then, on hearing the car outside, they get up and start barking. Their intention is to make us believe that they have been working hard, guarding the house in our absence. We treat them like replacement children, dogs who are not safe, home alone. We are just big softies with those boys; I think we spoil them more than we did the children when they were younger. My guilt surges at the thought of that fact. We rationalise this to ourselves with the fact that it is not safe to leave them yet. Therefore, we set off for another noisy trip. Both boys will bark for the entire journey. Buster barks at every vehicle he sees or hears, whilst Dave barks at Buster. We have our lists divided into essential items to buy, and a list of emails and messages, which need a response. We head to the free internet in the McDonald's restaurant in nearby St Junien.

As we enjoy our long awaited cups of hot coffee, which help to warm our bones after sleeping on the floor, our visit to complete our email admin comes to an abrupt end. The laptop battery runs out of power, adding another item to the things to do at home list. Listing has become an obsessive-compulsive necessity. Jet lag and excitement, tinged with concern for Jaime, is consuming my mental capacity and memory abilities. Therefore, the new list of things to do at home starts with; find the Australian to French adapter that is in our suitcase somewhere. No doubt, we will find it concealed inside one of my boots or another hollow packing space. This particular to do item is essential, as we need the laptop fully charged for tomorrow. We still need to update the children of our whereabouts, confirm our details with the utility companies and start researching local renovation supplies.

The internet admin to do list starts with priority emails:

1. Email or Facebook all the children (this may take a while I feel copy and paste coming on!)

2. Email the English speaking EDF (Électricité de France) service provider to set up our contract. We are fortunate that the electricity is connected and working, but we need to ensure it stays that way!

We know that it will be some time before we can get a telephone line or the internet installed. There has never been a telephone line at the property. Therefore, installation will need a pole erected and some expensive connection and engineer fees. For the immediate future, we will become resourceful locators of free Wi-Fi around the towns and villages. Revived by our coffee and food, yet frustrated by the de-charged laptop, we do the shopping we need and head home. The shopping items come from a list of essential equipment/items for our new living arrangements. Despite the need to take care when spending, some items are necessities and not luxuries. In hindsight, despite our research, our naivety about the cost living and DIY items in France is laughable. Our meagre eight thousand euros budget is not all earmarked for the renovations. We need to set up the basics to live, and secure a patch repair for the roof. The added pressure is that this money has to keep us afloat until Nigel or I find work, or until I receive payment for my writing articles. We consider with great scrutiny every piece of expenditure. We review its necessity in the short term and it usefulness in the medium and long term. It is a vulnerable state to be in whilst neither of us has any paid work.

Our first experience of French shops, with only minimal French language skills to lean on, was always going to test us. However, we survive and, like excited kids, we return home after buying the basics we need to set up our base 'glamp camp.' We start the formidable task of making our home habitable. Are we really going to attempt to live in here whilst we restore it to a degree of its former glory? Of course we are, 'glamping' Butfield style. We are good at this; remember reading about our adventures living in the woods in outback Queensland, Australia? If we did that, we are capable of anything! The dictionary definition of glamping is, 'a form of camping with accommodation and facilities, more luxurious than those associated with traditional camping. Glamping is likely to satisfy any city slicker seeking a little refuge in nature without foregoing any of life's luxuries.' I think that just about describes our situation. There is a toilet, albeit with no privacy, installed in the cave. We have a sink with one tap in the living area on the landing, and the roof, which has a section missing. At least it is intact over the part of the house where we currently live. With the added luxury of electricity, we tick enough boxes to qualify as glampers I think. We packed two camping plates and mugs in our suitcase so with today's new additions are things are improving. We now have two knives and forks, but no spoons, as they were not on the list!

Internet and coffee take two.

With the laptop battery recharged, we are ready to undertake our missions for today. We take the boys in their sky crates with us again today, as we do not know how long we will be out for, well that is today's excuse.

We make our way to Hyper U and Le Clerc in St Junien. Both of these stores sell a mixture of household items, everyday food and domestic items as well as small items of furniture. We spot a small fridge for ninety-nine euros in Hyper U, but decide to check prices elsewhere before buying it.

Our digestive systems are in free fall, not knowing what to expect next. In total, we endured thirty-six hours of inflight meals, and then sandwiches and fruit on arrival day. Convenience foods, requiring the addition of boiling water, followed as the nearest thing to a cooked meal. Therefore, today's necessity item to buy is a small tabletop electric cooking appliance, which has a small oven and two hob rings. A kettle and some precious spoons for my coffee are also on the list for good measure. This may appear meagre, but our kitchen belongings from Tasmania will arrive in three to four months. We do not want to waste money on duplicate items so we will make do and mend, as my mum used to say.

The rain that greeted us on arrival in Paris continues into day three of our French life. Our roof is leaking from various places, so we position our newly acquired plastic buckets below the leaks. These buckets, mine is bright pink, will also double as the receptacles to have a daily strip wash in the absence of a hand basin or bathroom.

For the second time, we forget about the infamous two-hour French lunch break. Everything closes, including the bricolage (hardware store) which we need for essential DIY supplies. We walk the streets of Chabanais looking and acting like tourists. As we stand near the bridge, we admire the mill pool stillness of the Vienne River to the right of the bridge, as you look towards Chirac. This is in contrast to the white water rapids on the left as the water descends at speed over rocks and fallen trees.

We are glad to have made it back whilst we still have enough daylight to do some work indoors. To start with, we do some heavy duty cleaning and clearing of debris within the house. As we brush down the cobweb-laden walls and beams, and sweep the oak floors which have years of dust and dirt on them, the time soon passes. I talk a lot, as anyone that knows me will tell you. As I sweep I talk about how many old skin cells, mice droppings, etc., must be present in the dirt and dust accumulating at the top of the stairs. This all becomes too much for Nigel, who decides he has outdoor work to investigate to make the garden fit for the boys.

When he returns he finds a task which needs his 'total concentration.' It is code for 'it's time for you to stop talking to me.' His task is preparing and painting the walls in what will be our bedroom. When Nigel starts something, he has to complete it. The preparations and painting continue late into the evening using the light of our solitary bulb. He is a man on a mission. Immediately the first coat is on, he is not happy with the quality of French paint or the brushes. We will later discover that many British expats pay for paint deliveries from the UK. They prefer this to using an inferior quality, expensive, French paint.

While Nigel continues painting he moans. I attempt to set up our living area, which is quite a task with no furniture or dry places to put things. We are using the paint tins as chairs instead of the air mattress as we have applied a puncture repair patch. Fingers crossed for the air mattress staying inflated tonight.

My kitchen!

Tonight, on our new cooker, we prepare and consume a feast of fresh vegetables. After eating airplane meals and pot noodles for the last few days this tastes amazing. We check the air mattress before we relax onto it after dinner. Note to self - we need some chairs, something else for the list tomorrow; I am too old to sit this low down after eating. Before we have enjoyed our first glass of wine, we are deflating. Well not us literally, but the air mattress on which we are sitting. Have we punctured somewhere else or is it a leaky valve? After further investigation, we decide it is a valve issue, and after some twisting and pushing to secure it, we inflate it again and hope for the best. We bought a pillow for Nigel today so, air mattress permitting; a better night's sleep awaits us. We need the sleep, as another hectic day tomorrow awaits us.

Despite our reluctance to spend, we discover things that we need in order to attempt some of the tasks around the house. Our daily list grows. After another night of disturbed sleep on our air mattress, we both have crippling backache. We decide that two plastic garden chairs, at ten euros each, are a worthwhile investment. Nigel reminds me that I need to take care with the chairs. I have a well-earned reputation for breaking or falling through camping or outdoor chairs. It is a long-standing family joke. I sit on one of the chairs as we buy them in the bricolage store, I never realised I could miss a chair so much. Since our arrival, we have drunk coffee and eaten our meals, supported by any available wall and sitting on a paint pot. Outside in the garden we sit on an upturned bucket, so having a chair is bliss.

After the recent events with our air mattress failing us, we decide that having a comfortable place to sleep is now a necessity and not a luxury. Each day we work from eight in the morning until seven in the evening, and we eat our lunch on the go, unlike the French. The need for a good night's sleep is paramount for us to complete the physical hard work on the renovations, while finding our way through the French bureaucracy requires patience and perseverance. To rationalise buying the bed even further, we will need a spare bed for a guest room in October when Jaime visits. Decision made; it is not an extravagance.

The act of buying a sofa bed, after debating the decision to buy it now, means addressing the language barrier to get what we want. In the Le Clerc store, the furniture assistant speaks no English. Undeterred Nigel uses his international finger rubbing sign for money. I assist with the French to English dictionary, and we buy the sofa bed for two hundred euros. A younger female assistant is given the task of removing the sofa bed from the store display and delivering it to our car. She arrives with a miniature pallet mover, over which she has little, and at times no, control. Nigel offers to carry it out, but she is insistent she must move it. Once outside, the blue concrete pillars that stop cars blocking the exit now halt her pallet-moving machine. We now have to carry the sofa bed to the car after all. Excited at the prospect of a good night's sleep we overlook the small matter of having no bed linen. Never mind, sleeping bags will suffice.

Dave and Buster wait patiently for Nigel to carry the mattress up from the car: Guess who will be sitting in comfort first?

CHAPTER 3 LA GRANDE TOMATE

French encounters
As the boys cannot yet run free in the garden, we walk them to the village green twice a day. There they can run freely off the lead and play with the ball. Watching them practice their synchronised well-choreographed routine is amazing. It appears no one else frequents the village green, which is a shame because it is beautiful, but it is great news for our boys. On their afternoon walk, we have our first formal encounter with three of our French neighbours. Andre, Janine and Yvette all look as if they are in the sixty years plus age group. They do not speak any English but, undeterred, we try to interact from the beginning. We will not shy away from our neighbours because of the language barrier.

"Bonjour. Je m'appelle Sarah, et Nigel. Vous, vous appelle comment?" I say in my 'pigeon French,' a term meaning English speaking people attempting to converse with limited French language skills.

I am telling them who we are and asking their names. This question gets us off to a great start even if they are already laughing politely, probably at my pronunciation. We use the English to French dictionary, which Janine hastily obtains from her kitchen windowsill. It is as though she prepared for this encounter, and we manage to exchange names and introduce our boys, Dave and Buster. Feeling a little flustered after this brief encounter, I know it is exactly what we need to do to learn the language. However, I feel glad to be heading home when it is over.

"You were awesome." Nigel whispers as we walk towards our barn door. "That means so much to me. Thank you, Sweetheart."

With beautiful evening sunshine and a clear sky, we decide to light the enormous bread oven, situated outside our back door. I wonder if Madame Marchand was the baker for the whole village. The bread oven is big enough to sleep in. Ah ha, there's a thought, it might be warmer than in the house.

Our aim is to see if we can bake jacket potatoes for a late dinner while clearing more of the vegetation in the garden. All looks well until the oven starts producing huge amounts of smoke, which appears to come from our roof and looks alarming. On further inspection, it appears that there is no external flue or chimney connected to the oven, so we extinguish the fire. We will need to do some further investigation and maintenance work before our next attempt at cooking al fresco. Undeterred we chop the warm potatoes into 'pomme frites,' that is French fries or chips to us expats, and fry them indoors. We serve them with mussels in a garlic sauce for our Friday night fish and chip supper. Our energy seems limitless now; however, I think it is excitement and adrenaline. Whatever it is, we are thriving on it.

In the house, application of the second coat of paint in the bedroom continues, and it now looks clean. Nigel's work has transformed the walls. It takes them from off-white surfaces, whose peeling flakes resemble sunburnt skin, and transforms them into a matt white slightly uneven canvas. The cobweb covered walls that greeted us only a few days ago are a distant memory now. The lintel beam above the bedroom window now sports a coat of shiny black gloss paint. It looks rustic, similar to a feature in a quaint Cornish fisherman's cottage. However, it gives the long narrow window some much need definition.

Dave is determined not to stand on a wet floor!

My job today is to scrub the oak wood floors for the first time; the wash water, which I have to change three times, resembles chocolate milk. These floors are going to be glorious when they have had several bouts of scrubbing and eventually some sanding and varnish. Mantra whilst I scrub 'There is a nice floor beneath this dirt.'

We need a roofer urgently; the rain continues to ingress, soaking the oak roof beams and the contents of the barn. Two areas leak indoors, and the initial devis (quote,) for a total roof repair is more than the cost of the house. I doubt we will even afford a patch repair at this rate. With no income, we will have to choose with care what money we spend and where. The entrance to the barn from the back garden is inaccessible due to randomly placed pieces of wood and an overgrown grape vine and to prise it open is not going to be as simple as we had hoped. Barricaded up as if preventing an invasion, an array of old pots and rags, plastic sacks full of rubbish and a mound of rubble defend the entrance to our barn. The barn is equal in area to the actual house. Undeterred we plough through, and eventually the door opens. However, it only has one hinge working so it hangs like a flag on a pole.

Now the real work begins. The view from the barn door resembles a scene from the film 'Secret Garden.' Our grape vine hangs above us with an overabundance of green grapes heavy and plump. In my viewfinder, the overgrown haven, aka our garden, requires some much-needed tender loving care.

My ten French language lessons in Tasmania with Murielle really paid off today, as we went to Hyper U to buy the fridge we had spotted on our last visit. Completing the purchase called for our personal details for the facture (guarantee.) My role is to give our telephone number to the assistant. Therefore, my knowledge of French numbers came to the fore again, taking me back to my school day French lessons with Mrs Owers. I was never any good at French at school so I do not know why I thought I could learn it now over thirty years later.

"Mon numéro de téléphone est-zéro, quatre, huit, sept, trois, quatre, zéro, sept, quatre, deux." This combination of words stumble from my mouth in a slow yet controlled tone.

The assistant stands and looks at me, his face frozen, no smile or movement. In an instant, I remember the other part of the numbers French lesson; the French do not say the numbers one at a time they say them in twos. Therefore, I should have said "zero quatre, quatre-vingt sept, trente-quatre, zero sept, quarante-deux." Before I have a chance to redeem myself with a second attempt, he gestures to the keypad for me to type it in. The now well-rehearsed phrase, 'J'habite, Le Bourg, Chirac,' also comes in useful today to confirm our address. As usual, the assistant insists on transporting the fridge alone out to the car, despite having half of one arm missing. He also speaks no English.

What a day. Then to top it off we receive a telephone call to say we need to pay the 'Pack and Send' parcel company invoice online immediately. Therefore, we need to log on to the internet from the car park outside Café Clemence in Chabanais. Our boxes, all thirty-one of them, collected from John, Nigel's father, in Tasmania can now start their journey. Now that the exact weight and size of our consignment is known, the charges are calculated, and as soon as we have paid, they can be shipped. The cost will be AUD $1725 to get them to Lyon, France. The plan is that we will then hire a van, go and pay the customs charges and bring our belongings home. However, that is a long way off as they are travelling by sea and not due to arrive for three to four months.

With the chill of autumn in the air, and the knowledge that winter is approaching, we decide to buy a wood burner. There is already a working chimney, so that is a good start. At the bricolage store in Chabanais, we enlist the help of an assistant, who turns out to have limited English skills. Together we manage to find a wood burner and the chimney lining that we need. Three meters of this thick snake like tubing is going to be an expensive lining to put up a chimney where no one can see it. At the till, whilst processing the payment, the assistant gestures to the cashier. He waves a poster that came from the front of the display wood burner that we were purchasing. The cashier types in the details. Some animated pointing and hand gestures accompanied by loud discussions in French follows. It is something to do with the picture of a pot plant on the poster that indicates a free gift is on offer. After paying, Nigel heads outside with the wood burner and the assistant. Inside, I am presented with our free gift, two very small toffee sweets, not the pot plant I anticipated. We did chuckle about it though, and we needed those sweets for the next stage of this operation. Maybe the staff knew what lay ahead for us. The wood burner weighs 103 kg. Nigel and the young male assistant are just about to lift the wood burner into the hire car when frenzied French shouting ensues, appearing to come from a senior assistant. He begins gesturing to the young assistant to stop. The senior assistant, who could be the manager, comes out and lifts the wood burner with Nigel instead. He is obviously trying to protect the young lad from injury. As it turns out this is the easy bit. Nigel and I now have to carry it upstairs when we get home. The wood burner, with its black matte finish is perfect, I cannot wait to see our first fire alight, but it will not be today.

We are still using our Telstra Australian mobile phones as the task of acquiring French ones has yet to top our priority list. Before we left Australia, our eldest daughter Samantha gave us her old UK Orange mobile to try if needed. However, with limited mobile network in the house I walk down the road to try to top it up. I am using an Australian credit card and as soon as I give an Australian address, the operator starts passing me from pillar to post. I abandon this mission for today and put it in the non-urgent category.

The next task

Nigel's self-appointed task now is to install the wood burner. In a successful, yet painful manoeuvre for both of us, we carry it upstairs. Nigel removes the door and as many of the components as he can to reduce the weight. To be honest I think we only reduced by about five kilograms, but it all helps. Our main concern is that the total weight on the staircase during this challenge is going to be over 250 kg. Will it hold the wood burner and us? There is only one way to find out.

It did. The first stage of the challenge is now complete, but not without us sustaining injuries. Nigel has bruises on his knee from trying to support the weight, whilst I move backwards up the stairs still holding on for dear life. I have a bruise on my foot after I failed to remove it in time, meaning it became wedged between the burner and the staircase. There are three further fast developing bruises on my right arm after it too found itself in the wrong position. Nevertheless, the burner is now upstairs and in position. Another trip to the bricolage store in Chabanais follows after we realise that we need a heat protective ledge before the installation commences. After a lot of thinking, and hard work the flue is in place and the wood burner is ready for action. We will test it tonight after all.

Reflections

Our new French way of life with all its quirks and idiosyncrasies feels calm and organised, despite our current living conditions. It is an exquisitely, warm sunny day, despite being the last week in September, exactly the way you would imagine a day in rural France. Sitting on an upturned bucket outside the back door, I marvel at the simplistic beauty of Europe that I have missed whilst living in Australia. The sun, shining through the alder trees, casts its shadows on the neatly cut lawns of the non-resident British neighbours to my right. The well cared for vegetable gardens of the French neighbours to my left look splendid. The sky is clear blue, not a cloud in sight, and the only disturbance to the vibrant blue is the white snaking trails of aircraft passing by high above. The pigeons take to the high trees near the brook, while the blue tits and blackbirds enter our airspace and, as if on autopilot, take up their positions in the barn, the grape vines and the compost heap. They appear completely oblivious to the new inhabitants of this previously empty dwelling that provides their food and shelter.

Today the church bells ring at eight o'clock in the morning, twelve noon and seven o'clock in the evening. I ponder why it is different at the weekends. Later in the week, I discover my obvious oblivion during the daytime hours. When we are working hard on clearing decades of wood, rubble and unwanted belongings from the house and barn, I realise that the bells ring at these times every day of the week. In my curiosity over the significance of them, I prepare my questions about the bells, in French, for our neighbours. It will be a conversation topic, on our daily encounter when we walk the boys. On our Sunday morning walk with the boys, we meet Andre. As usual, he is working on his vegetable garden, a plot of land resembling a small paddock in size. We admire his work and he appears to express his dissatisfaction with this year's tomato crop. He shows us a rickety looking plastic bucket, with one side melted after obviously being too close to a bonfire at some stage. It contains cracked and splitting tomatoes in varying shades of yellow, orange, green and red. I attempt, in French, to say something along the lines of, 'You do well to maintain a vegetable patch of this size.' He holds his belly and laughs. I am not sure if I have said something completely different or inappropriate to that which I intended.

"J'ai quatre-vingt-cinq ans," says Andre.

When I hear him say these words, my brain furiously starts trying to work it out. In the meantime, Andre notices that Nigel has no idea of French numbers so he gestures with his fingers first showing eight and then five. Nigel nods and puts his thumb up as his gesture of comprehension. They shake hands, which we now know is Andre's sign for 'ok you understand now.'

Andre then walks away without saying 'au revoir,' which is most unusual. Even though we have only known him a few days, he is a polite and formally courteous man. We look at each other, unsure whether to stay or go as the conversation had not ended in his normal polite French fashion. Therefore, we wait. Andre proceeds to pick some yellow smaller tomatoes and two huge red tomatoes, which looked like a mutation of three tomatoes in one.

"La grande tomate!" Andre booms proudly as he hands over the tomato medley.

"Oui, merci," I reply taking hold of the misshapen fruits.

"Grande!" Nigel says in his best French accent, which sounds like he is clearing his throat.

Andre seems to give us instructions to put them in the sun, 'soleil' to ripen them. When we get home, Nigel cannot resist taking a photograph. He positions them against an old barrel and a boot that I found in the garden to demonstrate their enormity and irregular appearance.

After their walk, the boys enjoy lying in the sun while we return to work on the house and garden. They are not overly happy at not being able to run free. They are cattle dogs after all, but for now, as we have no dog fence it is the only safe way for them to be in the garden. There are many feral cats in this area, which the boys are keen to chase. The feral cats that frequent our garden are a new concept for the boys. Cats are not popular in Australia. They are perceived to be the main contributory factor in the demise of many small animal species over the years. For the boys, if it moves it is fair game, and they would chase the cats forever, with stamina any iron man would admire.

CHAPTER 4 IS SHE OK TO BE LEFT THERE ALONE?

Three of my four children utter these words when we announce that Nigel will be returning to the UK within ten days of our arrival. His mission is to buy a car, see some of the children and collect some essential provisions. These include Marmite, gravy, horseradish sauce and pickled onion monster munch. Moreover, who is 'she,' the cat's mother?

Sunday, a day of rest. There is no chance of that, living and working in our Chirac renovation boot camp. At least we are able to enjoy our first Sunday in France together before Nigel leaves. He wants to ensure that everything is secure and that there is no need for me to go into the barn whilst he will be away for a week. Part of this preparation is to make off road parking for our car, which Nigel will bring back with him. Work comes to a halt for further investigation of a potentially gruesome discovery. Whilst clearing the fallen roof tiles from our picture window, as we now call our hole in the roof, I find a plastic bag containing what appears to be rubbish. It is on top of the dilapidated chicken coop and appears to contain an assortment of old newspapers. I intend collecting any pieces of newspaper or memorabilia with old dates on them to make a framed collage of our renovation discoveries, so I have to look inside.

"Quick, get here!"

"What have you done now?" Nigel shouts as he rushes in, expecting that I have fallen, tripped or done any one of the clumsy things I do on almost a daily basis. We both peep into the bag and then stare at each other. I know my mouth is doing a grimacing mouth action like Wallace in the Wallace and Gromit films. Inside is what resembles human hair in a tidy plait. Attached to it is something more sinister in appearance. It looks like a fragment of decaying dried tissue, which resembles pigskin, or skull tissue.

"Gross!" Nigel says as he releases his grip on the bag.

Ever the nosey woman and ex nurse, who has seen many body parts in varying degrees of health and decay, I open the bag for further investigation. My first clinical observation is that it does not smell, unusual if it were skin or flesh. The hairpiece, obviously made from real hair, is in a tight, neat braid, circled into a bun. I hold onto the brittle tissue, and let the braid hang down to its full length of about ten inches. From inside, a small, yellow ribbon bow attached to a ringlet of hair and two smaller ringlets, drop out. They look as if they should hang in front of each ear, like a hairstyle from an adaptation of a Jane Austen Novel. When we next go to the internet or the library, I will investigate the origins of this hair accessory. I plan to keep my find, but Nigel says it cannot come into the house. So for now my box of intriguing finds and treasures is confined to the barn.

We stop for lunch just as a bicycle rally passes by and branches off towards the green. Today, apparently, it will cover 50 km including Chirac, Chabrac, Exideuil and Chabanais. I am glad we are not over there with the boys off the lead; they would enjoy chasing the bikes for the complete 50 km, snapping at their wheels. Shortly after this, we hear the now unfamiliar sound of sirens. When we lived in Hobart, Tasmania before moving to France, the sound of some form of emergency service vehicle was commonplace. I am already used to the intensity of the peace and quiet here in our rural idle. Therefore, the sound of the Gendarmes (police) makes me curious to find out what is happening; I say I am curious, Nigel says I am nosey. I am quick to open the shutters in our upstairs, makeshift kitchen area. We stick our heads out and strain to see where the sound of the sirens is coming from; it appears to be coming from the church. Then we spot two motorcycle Gendarmes blocking off the road for a convoy of motorcycles, I think some are Harley Davidsons. The motorcycles pass through, exiting from the lane behind the church, which is a back route from Exideuil to the main road leading to Confolens. The convoy lasts for at least five to ten minutes with lots of noise and horn sounding. The boys bark loudly from the back garden, where they cannot see what is happening, but even so, they do not like it.

After a day of shovelling rubbish, clearing bricks and debris, we are pleased with our efforts. Nigel is eager to do the grand opening of our huge oak barn doors. I study the chalk, timeworn French handwriting, which is on the inner aspect of the door. It is a mixture of numbers and words, like a price list. Again, I fantasise about the last time anyone came in through them, either walking their livestock or pushing handcarts.

"Great, well that was a waste of time and energy."

This exclamation quickly brings me back to my senses. I glance across at the doors and can see no obvious obstacle to the grand opening.

"Are they stuck?"

"You could say that."

The two barn doors, unused for many years, now have a concrete path obstructing them. We assumed as the house faces directly onto the road that they would open inwards so as not to obstruct the road.

"Well that's this plan on hold until we can get an extension lead and the jigsaw out here to cut the doors shorter." Nigel says as he stomps off like a five year old to find another project to give him the 'Ta dah' moment he was expecting.

At the end of another sultry Sunday, we enjoy a glass of wine in the garden as we admire and discuss our day's efforts. Nigel again goes over the plans and logistics and the all-important list of things I am not to attempt while he is away. His major concerns are the intermittent network coverage of our mobile phones, my inability to speak French to summon help in an emergency and the fact that the neighbours do not speak English. The upshot is that pretty much all I can do is work on the garden or write.

Nigel asks me, "What will you do to entertain yourself in the evenings? We don't even have a television or radio."

"I have the boys, my writing, reading and sewing so I have plenty to do, don't worry."

"Will you be lonely?"

"Of course I will miss you, but I don't get lonely so don't worry."

I awake in the morning to discover that our payback for a relaxing evening in the garden, forgetting we are back in Europe with European insects, is three large gnat bites. Unconsciously I have been scratching them during the night. The result is that the one above my right eye makes my eye difficult to open. The two on my left hand mean I cannot hold anything due to my swollen fingers. Note to self - buy insect repellent and remember to use it. Why did I foolishly assume I could stop with all that now I am not in Australia? What an idiot I am sometimes.

Crazy English woman alone in rural France, God help them!

Monday: As Nigel sets off on his trip to the UK, he is excited about going to see Clair, Phillip and Laurence. He has planned his schedule with military precision. He leaves at eight o'clock in the morning to return the hire car to Limoges railway station. Then he will get a taxi to the airport for his Ryanair flight to Stansted. His coach, booked from Stansted to Colchester, takes him to his accommodation at the Red Lion Hotel, so everything is in place.

With many tasks planned for the time, I am alone I start in the garden. I plan to plant onions, garlic and spinach. My parsley, basil and lettuces are already growing in trays. They will transfer to my cold frame, which Nigel will build from some free old French windows we acquired. Once indoors, I clear out the back room of the house, destroying cobwebs and dust leaving a cloud in my wake. The oak floor, now swept and washed, has one corner that is different. The size of the floorboards varies, possibly from a repair at some point. Nonetheless, it now looks amazing. The window faces out onto our garden, and the sun shines into this room all day. I decide that as we have no furniture I will erect a makeshift table for my laptop.

I make it from bricks from the barn, and a piece of wood. I stole the idea from the garden bench Nigel erected for me at the weekend. Despite plagiarizing his idea, I am proud of my efforts. I sit in my fluorescent green plastic garden chair, typing up the first draft of my romantic fiction novel; this feels perfect.

From this window, I watch the morning mist disperse in the heat of the sun to reveal clear skies. In the distance, the free-range chickens pass their time roaming the grass-covered hills. I wonder where they lay their eggs? I love the peace and quiet here; it gives me inspiration and the ideas spill out onto numerous notepads. I even wake up in the night, with ideas, plots and changes. I think this increased creativity is due, in no small part, to the absence of external stimuli such as the internet and television. My mind is uninterrupted, free to explore and run with ideas; this is heaven.

The enjoyment of my period of quiet reflection is cut short by a sudden loud, crashing and rolling noise. A tractor with an oversized trailer of logs has arrived at my French neighbour Yvette's house while she is out. The cargo of logs is emptied in front of her open garage door. I wonder if this is intentional because when she returns she usually drives straight in. I know I cannot go and say anything that they would understand, so I just observe. I am now overcome with guilt because of my ignorance of the language.

On her return, Yvette parks beside the logs and walks across the road, returning with her wooden wheelbarrow. Within a few minutes, another car arrives; its passengers are a couple in their early fifties. They all then start to pile the logs into an assortment of wheelbarrows and move the logs into the barn. This activity took the industrious team most of the afternoon. I should tell you that Yvette, a widow, is only eighty-three years old!

I end my first day of solitude in the garden with the boys after their walk. It has been another beautiful warm day, so they welcome the cool refreshing cave area as we retire for the night.

Tuesday: It is raining just as Andre predicted yesterday; 'plui Mardi,' (rain Tuesday.) It remains humid, so I am still able to work outside on the garden. It is another busy day in the village. At nine o'clock, the continuous blowing of a car horn encourages my nosiness again. I see a van signed 'poissonnier.' I am quick to get my dictionary from the shelf and deduce that it is the fishmonger. Like a shy child at a new school, I spy from a distance as Yvette, Andre and Janine scuttle out to buy their provisions. They laugh and joke with the vendor before going back to their respective houses. I wish I were brave enough to go out, perhaps next time. When the van has left, I interpret the words I scribbled down that advertised his wares, fish, shellfish and crustaceans. I wonder how often he comes? It could be weekly. If so, I will keep an eye out next Tuesday for him. I may feel braver by then. I decide that today is the day to take on another brave task, my visit to the Maire's office. As a gesture of polite French etiquette, I need to go and introduce myself as the latest new member of the community, but I also need some questions answered. Armed with my pre-arranged questions in English, and in French, I attempt my missions:

How to apply, and obtain permission to erect a fence for the dogs?

To enquire about the frequency of the refuse collection.

How and where do I obtain some of the yellow recycle collection bags?

While thinking about and summoning up the courage to attempt this task, I have been dreaming about it on a regular basis. Last night I dreamt that I went to the Maire's office and that as I read my well-practiced questions in French, they asked me

"Why are you speaking like a character from Allo, Allo?"

Today, in reality, I walk into the office and the woman behind the counter is busy serving a French-speaking man. I pretend to peruse the notice board, none of which I can read. She immediately leaves him and comes to attend to me, making me somewhat embarrassed

"Bonjour, parlez-vous Anglais?" The words pour out of my mouth before my brain catches up. I now know that this is extremely rude on a first encounter.

"Petit peu; a little bit," she gestures with her thumb and forefinger in a pincer position. I chastise myself for thinking that she does indeed sound like the police officer in, 'Allo, Allo!' Why am I thinking this, when I should be concentrating on the task in hand? Stop it Sarah. I now need to stifle my amusement at her tone and refocus.

As it turns out her English comprehension and language is indeed petite. The foresight of my pre-scripted French questions and some help from the man at the counter, enables her to understand my queries. I discover that we do not need permission for a dog fence. I collect a year's supply of bags for recycling and the information on the refuse collection; my task is complete. I leave with my head held high, proud of my achievements. On a high from the success of my administration task, I decide to use the public telephone box to book an appointment with the roofer. This is not a challenge in real terms as he is English, but concern at the projected cost scares me from making the call. However, we have to find out. Karen, who works for Darren in the immobilier office in Chabanais, has recommended the roofer Tim Day. Tim agrees to come and view the hole in the roof next Tuesday on his way home from a nearby job. My meditation mantra now takes the form of: "Please be repairable for minimal cost until we can find some paid work here."

I make a cup of coffee as my reward for the successful completion of my bureaucratic task, almost spilling it down my front as another loud car horn noise erupts outside. This prompts me to stick my head out of the window again. The French will think I am nosey English woman. This time it is an unmarked white van outside Andre's house. I see Andre attend the van and come away with a baguette and a small loaf of bread. Ah, ha, the bakery van. I note the time and take note of where he goes next, which is up the slip road to the house on the hill opposite. It operates in a quick, no nonsense way. The transactions are efficient and smooth. No gossiping just buy the bread and go. As I return to my coffee I think to myself that, with these mobile services, I could survive here on bread and fish like in the bible. A sudden onset of nostalgia embraces me as I remember happy times whilst staying with my grandmother as a child. She suffered from chronic leg ulcers and so the majority of her provisions came from the mobile grocers. The visiting tradespeople would also take away her letters to post and her Littlewoods football coupon each week.

I manage to write two thousand words of my romance novel today; I am elated.

Wednesday: I decide to make my own bread today, as I am still not brave enough to attend the bread van. After translating the instructions on the yeast, I begin making what I hope will resemble a French baguette. However, as I have no weighing scales or measuring jug for the water a great deal of guess work goes into the mix along with the ingredients. Maybe I have a good eye, or I was fortunate to have the right combination of ingredients with a warm sunny aspect to encourage the bread to rise. Whatever the reasons the dough was perfect, as was the French bread I created. It didn't exactly resemble a French baguette, but it tasted delightful.

A hedge-cutting worker hinders dog walking today so the boys and I do a road walk instead on D 65 towards Chabrac. I walk and walk before realising I have no idea where I am going. As I am here alone and out walking with no mobile, which is not sensible and against Nigel's rules, I decide to head back. On the way, I spot the largest yellow and white pumpkins growing from a large compost pile near some storage buildings. Later in the year, I discover that these are the community pumpkins grown for decorating the village for Halloween.

With a sunny and hot afternoon ahead, I return to my gardening tasks. I plant two rows of onion bulbs, unsure if it is the right time as there are no instructions on the bag, and the label just says onions. Later I write an article for the Deux-Sevres Monthly: an English expat magazine in France. My article is due for publication in November, which makes me feel proud, but for now, I have no one to tell. I need a USB stick, as the vulnerability of writing on the laptop and not backing up is overwhelming. Nigel has promised to bring me some back.

Thursday: I love the mornings here in France. As it gets light I open the shutters and the windows, and the fresh air is exhilarating like a dose of energy for the day. I prepare and eat my breakfast of homemade bread with a boiled egg, utilising the top of the water container as an eggcup. Whilst looking out over uninterrupted views of the meadows to the back of our house a sense of calm ensues, and for a few moments, I lose myself in the serenity of the scene.

I walk the dogs this morning and have my now daily chat with Andre, who reveals he owns the garage/barn attached to our barn. Yvette owns the vegetable garden at the back of it, which is next to our garden. I wonder why he is telling me this until Andre indicates that he can see from his barn that I have a big hole in the roof of my barn. I smile to myself, 'Does he think I don't know it's there?' I am still chuckling to myself as I arrive home. You can see the hole in the roof from the inside and outside of the barn.

So today I think I have the timings of the bread van sorted, and I intend go out with my money and my bread order prepared. However, the van comes two hours early and from a different direction catching me out again.

It comes from Confolens instead of Chabanais. Andre and Janine have gone to the Chabanais market, so there are only a few customers for the bread van today. Yvette goes out with her red bread bag with a big white flower on the side. I decide to give up on this whimsical idea of buying bread and concentrate on my writing. Lo and behold, at eleven thirty, another bread van comes from Chabanais and Andre is back just before, so they still buy their bread. Missed it again.

Nigel is catching the night ferry home tonight at eleven o'clock. I cannot wait to see him.

Friday: Nigel's ferry is due to dock at eight o'clock this morning; he then has a seven-hour drive home. It is a sunny day, nice weather for Nigel's return. With my writing complete, this morning I sit outside in the sun and work on mind mapping the future chapters. The new ending that I have written excites me, just writing it makes me cry. I hope the readers feel the same emotion when they read it.

Nigel arrives home at three o'clock. It is so good to see him. Our car, a second-hand blue Peugeot 406 estate, will be our workhorse from now on, helping us obtain supplies for our renovation. I am like a kid at Christmas going through the Tesco bags of treats, including horseradish sauce and gravy granules. We are so typically British. We sit outside in the sun talking and I enjoy listening to the news of the children he met up with on his trip. A perfect day.

When I first walked the boys while Nigel was away, Andre and Janine were concerned that Nigel was missing. They assumed he was, 'malade,' ill or sick. I told them he was in England visiting the children. Each day they asked if I was sad, at being alone. They would imitate crying by rubbing their eyes, which was quite comical.

"Non, d'accord." No, I am okay, I said each time.

On the first dog walk after Nigel's return, Andre tells Nigel I was crying all the time he was away. Maybe they wanted to make sure he knew that I missed him.

At today's chat with Andre, he is out with his chainsaw tidying his garden for winter. He tells us today will be 'soleil' meaning sunny, which is good news as he picks us more green tomatoes and misshapen cucumbers to ripen. As we talk, Andre demonstrates his 'petit peu, Anglais' that he is learning from us. He can now say, "Okay, hello and goodbye," which is not bad for two weeks of informal training. He regularly laughs at our French pronunciation and often we all laugh together as we realise none of us understands the other. As the Deputy Maire walks by, he shakes hands with only the menfolk, as if I am invisible. He is also intrigued by our 'Australie deux chiens,' our two Australian cattle dogs. He too has "petit peu Anglais" and the conversation somehow moves onto mushrooms. We foraged some mushrooms this morning, but are unsure if they are edible. Nigel shows

Andre who says if the underside is 'rose' then it is okay to eat, but he warns us not to eat them if the underside is white. The Deputy Maire agrees, which is reassuring. We have read that if you eat poisonous mushrooms you notice no effects immediately, but sudden death can occur on the third day. Tonight we eat the mushrooms; if we are both alive on Friday, they were okay to eat!

CHAPTER 5 THE TEA TOWEL BANDIT STRIKES AS RENOVATIONS BEGIN

Togetherness, commitment, a sense of humour and self-belief are the qualities we bring to this latest adventure. As we start renovating a cottage in rural France, let the hard work begin.

Where do we begin? The whole house needs attention in some form, whether it is repairing the hole in the roof, or creating a floor above the trodden earth floor in the cave. The electrics, plumbing and layout all need attention. However, we need to be able to live in the house whilst we address the changes we want and need to make, thus adding a completely new dimension to the project. The easy, some would say sensible, option would be to rent a 'gite' (holiday cottage) nearby, get some contractors and get it done as quickly as possible. Back in the real world, our world, of keeping to a budget and family pressures, who can say what a realistic timeframe for this project is? We estimate that it will take three to five years to get the house how we want it. The act of owning and renovating a cottage as part of our French adventure is a big tick on our bucket list. In Australia, in the run up to moving, we spent hours looking at, and reading, home and garden magazines for ideas and inspiration. My folder of clippings is bulging, and I have not even started on the interior design. We have some features of the house that we want to restore as opposed to renovate. We aim to expose some of the interior stonewalls. There are granite and limestone blocks hidden beneath peeling render. They form the structure of the fireplaces on the landing and in the cave, and we know they will look amazing when exposed.

With this in mind, Nigel is chipping away at old render and damaged limestone in the hallway. Today he decides, half way through the task, that PPE (Personal Protective Equipment) might be a good idea. Clouds of dust gather despite having the windows open. It resembles a scene from a Snoopy cartoon when the character Pig Pen walks around with his cloud of dust and dirt following him. I walk in and find him wearing one of only three tea towels we own over his mouth and nose as a mask. I had to take a photograph because this is how his new nickname, the tea towel bandit originated. The tea towel bandit strikes again, as Nigel chips away at our feature wall of what will be the master bedroom, in the barn.

Whilst clearing some space for him to work in the barn, we find a wooden box. It has petal shaped holes in one side. It could be an old radio box or the decorative wood front to a cabinet. After putting it outside in the sun to dry out we discover a 1961 calendar nailed to the inside of the box. I prise it off and dry out the pages one by one, revealing maps of the local area. These included Angouleme, Confolens and a directory of Maire offices with telegraphic services for the whole of the Charente. There are hand written notes scattered throughout, obviously relating to someone's life. The notes appear to contain dates and monetary values, in Francs. Reading it feels intrusive, even though the notes are old and discarded. However, it is intriguing at the same time. I wonder who had written in the calendar, and to what the values relate. Is it wages, sales of produce or animals, expenditure or income? The mystery of the past, hidden in the very fabric of our little cottage, is slowly but surely revealing itself. We will frame the maps that form the directory, to display in the house, along with other handwritten notes and advertising signage found amongst the debris left to rot in the barn.

Throughout the house and barn, the tea towel bandit goes on to reveal large pieces of granite, and limestone blocks around the windows and doorways.

Today we start preparing the barn for the arrival of scaffolding, a momentous move forward in the quest to repair the huge hole in the roof. We salvage the tiles that remain intact after falling in when the roof apparently collapsed during heavy snow a few years before. As we pile up pieces of wood from the fallen purlins and rafters, we move what seem like thousands of pieces of roof tiles. Shovelling them into piles, we will use them as hard-core later. This preparation enables us to reveal the true extent of the roof repair mission ahead of us.

Underfoot the floor level is raised by at least four feet. This false floor consists of straw, composted over the years with animal excrement and rotting cardboard, wood and other debris. As we remove and transport it to the end of the garden in black buckets, my arms feel like they touch the floor as I walk. Fatigue from shovelling, carrying and walking up and down the garden hits, but we will not give in.

The floor in the barn needs to be clear and level for the scaffolding to be safe; therefore completing this task has a deadline that we have to meet. Despite being autumn the sun shines, and our exposed arms glistening with perspiration. In the absence of attending a gym since we moved, Nigel aims to make every renovation task an exercise routine so these tasks are perfect for him. Other exercise routines include shoulder pressing with oak beams and lifting granite boulders. Nigel pretends they are Atlas stones like the ones the contestants lift in the World's Strongest Man competitions. When he has to help me in the garden, we see extreme digging in action.

By November 2012, we have cleared and prepared the barn for Tim to start the mammoth task of making the roof safe, before starting to repair it. In true 'Good Life' barter style, Nigel exchanges his labour, despite his fear of heights and ladders, for a reduction on the cost of the repair. By mid-month, the work is progressing well. They build block work supporting walls from the loft floor level to the roof to support the roof beams, which are bowing and weather damaged from exposure to the elements, Tim likes attention to detail when it comes to following the natural line of the curved oak beams. The first block work wall goes up between our barn and Andre's garage next to it. It is an area which, until now, has had no support and just some scraps of wood nailed together to fill the gap. On the other side of the barn the block work wall they build will form a wall to our en-suite, when the upper level becomes our master bedroom.

We discuss our big, ambitious plans for the house and barn with Tim on many occasions over the first few months. He likes our plans, which is just as well because we are not changing them. The house will consist of an open plan kitchen, lounge and dining room on the ground floor, in what is now the cave. There will be a small cloakroom in the area under the stairs, which is currently the temporary bathroom. Upstairs, part of the landing will become the family bathroom and a walkway will link the two existing bedrooms. In the corner of Jaime's room, we will knock through to the barn with a door leading to my new office. My office will face the back of the house with three large windows above my desk. I will have wood floors, and Nigel can have an old leather armchair for him to sit in when he visits me. He becomes a book widower when I start writing and he likes to come and sit in the same room so we spend time together. There will be a four-step staircase up to our master bedroom on the mezzanine floor and an en-suite and walk-in dressing room built into the loft space over the house. Yes, I know, big ideas, but I always aim high and dream big. Nigel is learning so much from helping Tim with our roof and, after only a few weeks, he builds his first solo block work wall. The wall will be between our dining area and a temporary bathroom. He works hard to apply his newly acquired knowledge, and shapes the blocks to accommodate the branch like oak beams and uneven walls. We use our trusty Peugeot to get building supplies home from the bricolage store in St Junien. We buy twenty blocks at a time, which are then loaded into the back of the car until it looks like a boy racer's lowered XR3i, but without the alloys. The tyres look almost flat as we slowly make our way home. He also lays a concrete slab floor in the bathroom area, which makes the small space appear large enough for another project.

One of the projects that Nigel is dreading, because it involves plumbing, is installing a hand basin and taps. It may sound a little harsh to use the word dread, but that depends on your past experiences. Nigel dislikes plumbing with a passion based on his previous plumbing exploits. Whether it is putting in a new washing machine or hooking up the cold-water feed to a drinks dispenser in the fridge, something always leaks. The plumbing here is old, and the sizes do not correspond to any fittings you can buy at the bricolage. Therefore, this project which involves installing a mixer tap is not going to be a straightforward task. With no hot water boiler, he manages to connect the cold-water feed, after the usual cursing and vowing never to touch the plumbing again. However as the wall to the barn, is one meter thick we are unable to drill through to connect the waste pipe. Therefore, the sink waste will drain into an old paint bucket for now. Nigel's problem with that is my forgetfulness and clumsiness. The floor has been awash with dirty wash water more times that I care to admit.

It is also during November 2012, in the midst of renovation activity, that Julia and Phil invite us to dinner. As it is before our boxes arrive from Australia, we do not have a big choice of clothes for social occasions. Nigel brought one shirt in our suitcase, and it remains there. We do not own an iron or ironing board yet. We try hanging the shirt up for a week but it remains full of deep creases. I decide to improvise when Nigel is not looking, in case a disaster occurs. I use the wood burner to heat the crepe frying pan. Our makeshift table is made from an old door taken down in the cave, which lies on legs made of bricks from the partition wall we demolished. I set up my ironing area on it. Laying a towel on the table and using a wet tea towel for the steam effect, I rub the shirt creases with my crepe pan for well over an hour. Nigel, pleased by my efforts, feels comfortable wearing the shirt, even though it is not ironed to his normal military standard of ironing perfection. That evening he tells Phil about my ironing technique and Phil calls us 'legends,' a term I will never forget.

As the winter of depression looms, on 6th December 2012 Nigel gives Tim a call to tell him we need to slow down the roof repairs due to our lack of money. 2013 starts with our renovation work on hold, many projects hanging in the balance, unable to progress further until we save some money. Once Nigel is working, we decide that each week we will spend twenty to fifty euros on building supplies. Twenty euros will buy twenty building blocks, a couple of sheets of marine ply plasterboard for the bathroom or four lengths of wood to build studwork walls. Even on a budget, we will keep the work moving forward through 2013. I admit that we have made some schoolboy errors, on this steep learning curve, one of mine being an attempt to buy paint. A simple enough task; buy a tin of white paint. I see the word 'blanc' meaning white on a tin that looks exactly like the ones Nigel has been using. Back at home, I prise open the lid, passing it to Nigel who is ready with his paintbrush.

"It's a bit thick," he says.

"Give it a stir, it'll be alright"

No amount of stirring helps and the paint has a gritty texture. Nigel has already daubed some on the wall. He picks up the tin.

"Crepi, that's not the word for paint, it's peinture."

We find out later from Tim that 'crepi' is a textured wall covering for disguising uneven surfaces. It is a mix of emulsion paint and sand, a similar product to Sandtex in the UK. It does not cover any large deficiencies in your stone or brickwork, but will cover small cracks. Not wanting to waste this new product in our DIY store Nigel uses a trowel to apply it to the ugly red bricks on the chimney breast. The white textured finish enhances the appearance of the two limestone pillars beneath.

In this fashion, our renovation work continued throughout the year. With various visits due from the children between March and October, certain aspects of the renovation become a necessity instead of luxury. Some projects jump the queue in the priority list. These include replacing our tarpaulin bathroom door with a wooden one for some privacy, and building a utility room, complete with a sink and draining board, in the barn.

On 14th October 2013, Nigel builds a wooden, raised framework and floor over the sloping trodden earth surface in the cave. The transformation of the space is astonishing. The floor space looks vast, bright and appealing to the eye. It is easy to take for granted the way things look when you live with them day in day out. To have a flat surface to walk on and to be able to lay down a rug is an awesome sensation. Now it looks like a home.

On 27th November 2013, a momentous day in the renovation schedule arrives. We finally have a bath installed complete with hot water tank. It has only taken fourteen months to get at this stage, which I think is pretty good considering our financial situation. Nigel did a day's free labour in exchange for a second-hand hot water tank. He attaches it to the wall above the bath. The bath he bought for sixty-five euros from an Angouleme bricolage store, during a sale. We have no taps for the bath so when it is bath time he uses his spanner and a piece of flexible piping to fill it. After filling the bath with hot water, he then ferries many kettles of cold water to get it to the right temperature. Bush mechanics it may be, but after a hard day's work on the house, to be able to sit or lay in the bath feels awesome. As each small piece of the renovation puzzle falls into place, it becomes easier to visualise the way our home will look on completion.

CHAPTER 6 A BOOMERANG NAMED JAIME

From Glass Half Full: Our Australian adventure.

We drove into the car park; my heart started racing, so much so that I felt faint. Just seeing him standing there, leaning on his car, was all it took. Despite not seeing him for years, I recognised his stance and demeanour; it was Jack. Nigel pulled up alongside him, and we all got out. For Jaime, this must have been a strange scenario because he essentially was a stranger, even though they 'chatted' on Facebook in the run up to today. She did not 'know' him. For Jaime's sake alone, Nigel made small talk, for which I felt extremely grateful; I could not speak. I tried to hold back my tears as I held her tightly and said goodbye. My heart was breaking again just as it did when he took Molly.

Jaime whispered, "I love you mummy."

That short sentence opened the floodgates of tears and emotions pent up inside. I forced myself to turn my head as the tears fell furiously. I had promised Jaime I would not cry. Jack ushered Jaime into the back of the car, and I left Nigel to say goodbye. I could not look back. I did not know when I would next see her, although we planned to speak the following day, and she promised to text me when they got home to the UK.

Since that fateful day of handing over Jaime to Jack there has been a hole torn in my heart. The last time I experienced this was when he stole Molly away from me at only four months of age. I ached to hold Molly, to see her and hear her; and yet here I was allowing him now to do it again, albeit Jaime was a seemingly willing participant on this occasion. She made this decision, which would break my heart; whether it was under his influence didn't matter. This ache in my heart remained unchanged regardless of who, or what was to blame. The fear for her safety remained although I had to assume for my own sanity that at sixteen, she was more capable of protecting herself than a four-month-old baby would have been. Nigel did not understand my feelings. The bond between him and Jaime seemed irreparably broken now. It had been since the day she announced she was going to go to live with Jack, her biological father and the person I had protected her from for sixteen years. Nigel could hardly look at her. It was like a slap in the face, for all the years he spent as the one and only father figure, dad, daddy she ever knew and loved. Jaime had no concept of the level of hurt her decision caused and once again, I was playing referee in a battle of wills.

With Jaime in Britain, Nigel relaxed into French life with just the two of us. Although I enjoyed the feeling of togetherness as a couple, as we had never experienced any time living alone together since we met in 1997, as a mother I was empty inside. It may have felt easier if I believed and trusted that Jack would care for and love Jaime as much I do. However, I knew deep down there was no love for her. It was revenge, point scoring. He had already stolen one beautiful daughter and now he had them both. I had no mental space remaining to conduct the immature battles with him anymore. I had to move on. However, my intuition or maternal instinct told me that something would happen and that it would only be a matter of time. Jaime lingered in my thoughts. Even though she texted me as promised, the night she left, she did not say much. I had to carry on with my life waiting and hoping that God listened to my prayers and watched over her for me.

The next chapter for Jaime

Even though before we left Australia Jaime reached school leaving age having completed her schooling in Hobart, Tasmania, in the UK she was not yet old enough to leave school. Therefore, Jack had to enrol her in a nearby high school. For Jaime this in itself was an ordeal, since she had dyslexia and dysnumeric issues. Without the support she received in Australia, very quickly Jaime was feeling threatened and unhappy in the school environment. Of course, Jack, being of very low intellect himself, could not relate to her problems. Nonetheless, she persevered, and I felt proud that she at least was trying to make an effort. However, she was not being made as welcome as she hoped and expected. She had no bedroom at Jack's house; she slept on a sofa bed in the lounge. Therefore, she had to wait until Jack, his current girlfriend, Molly and any of the other visiting siblings, of which there were many, had gone to bed before she could go to sleep. The result of this sleep deprivation, stress at school and the poor diet she was now eating was a recipe for personal disaster for Jaime. Eating fast food and ready meals, something we never ate in Australia, meant she was gaining weight rapidly. The frustration at her now spotty appearance and ill-fitting clothes fuelled the fire of teenage trauma, which she was enduring.

Jaime's Visit

Unaware of the full extent of her current situation, I make plans for Jaime to visit us in France for the October half term school holidays. I book the flights and make ready a room in our renovation-building site for my little girl. We have bought a second hand bed from the reclamation yard, borrowed a mattress from an English expat neighbour and I am excited to show her our new project, a new family home.

When finally the day arrives to meet her at Limoges airport, the difference in her is shocking. Her puffy, spot sprinkled face, lank hair and lack of self-confidence as she walks across the tarmac with her head hung low, causes my tears to escalate. These tears initially of excitement at seeing her now turn to tears of fear for her wellbeing.

Two Dogs and a Suitcase

Mother and daughter reunited

Over the week that she is here, we have lots of good healthy food and we talk about ways she can help herself in her new environment. Despite wanting to say, "You are not going back," I know she has to decide for herself, or another big battle will consume us. This time I have to step back, bite my tongue and hope. It was a shock to discover that Jack just dropped her at Stansted Airport. He did not even go in to make sure her flight was on time, not cancelled, etc. Finding out while she is here that after dropping her at the airport he, his new girlfriend and Molly have jetted off to Turkey on holiday fills me with apprehension for Jaime's return to the UK. What if he is not there to meet her at Stansted? What if there is a delay in his flight from Turkey? So many scenarios to consider. However, I can do nothing other than ensure she has credit on her mobile phone and that her brother Rob in London is aware of the potential issues. I pray again.

When she arrives back in Stansted, true to form, he is not there, and she has to wait several hours. It is no surprise; I would expect nothing less from him. Despite this, Jaime wants to continue to try to form a bond with him, and once again, I need to respect her decision, for now that is.

However, within a week of her returning home to the UK, Jaime finds herself in the hospital with a relapse of her CRPS, (Chronic Regional Pain Syndrome) originally diagnosed in Australia. This relapse is the result of pain in her foot after knocking her toe. Jack, however, did the one thing that a parent of a child with CRPS should never do; he did not believe her. This act inevitably signalled the end for their relationship. After he accuses her of 'making it up for attention,' Jaime can see his true colours. Despite her being scared and in pain he does not stay at the hospital with her. Nigel and I never have and never would leave her alone like that. When I find out what is happening there is no question, I have to get there. I struggle to get a same day flight to be at her bedside. Eventually after a long wait at Limoges airport to find out if there are any 'no shows,' I pay 264 euros for a Ryanair flight that normally costs 19 euros.

On arrival at the hospital, I sleep beside her in the hospital bed, help with her physiotherapy and pain management sessions until five days later, she is fit to go home. Hoping that at last she will see that, if he would treat her like that, Jack does not care, I arrange for Jaime and me to stay at my sister Susie's in nearby Ipswich for a week. Again, Jaime decides to give him another chance.

As I fly back to France the pain in my heart intensifies. I know it sounds unbelievable, but there have been occasions when, while separated from my children, I have known, felt or sensed when they were suffering physical or emotional pain. I recognised this sensation and in my mind I knew this time, it was Jaime. Arriving back in France that night, I receive a distraught call from Jaime to say Jack has stolen her pain medication from her claiming she does not need it and that he needs it more. Prescription medications can be worth a lot in his unscrupulous world. There will be no second chances this time.

I am so angry, fearful and upset that I cannot find the words to talk to her. Then, despite the challenges of their relationship since she decided to stay with Jack, Nigel takes the phone from me and tells me to sit down. As I sit, the tears fall heavily onto our wooden floor.

"It is time to come home now, Jaime." Nigel slowly and calmly tells my sobbing and panic-stricken little girl on the other end of the mobile phone.

These events meant no more second chances could or would be given to Jack. My brother-in-law, Darren, collected Jaime, whom he found discarded at the side of the road with her bags and crutches. Jack did not even go outside to make sure she was safely collected. Anyone could have taken her. Darren took her home, and she stayed with my sister Susie and her family for a few days while she recovered enough to be able to walk without her crutches so that she could fly home to us. The Jaime and Jack episode was over.

CHAPTER 7 SURVIVING FRANCE

Soya to wild boar in three months

Well to be precise, from vegetables and soya protein to wild boar in one meal. How the worm has turned, as the Two Ronnie's would say. Up to now the house rules were no meat to be cooked or eaten in the house, a rule rigorously enforced when we lived in Hobart. For Samantha and Cam, the no meat rule was an especially harsh house rule when they were living with us. It caused them to eat out a couple of times a week to get their meat fix.

Nigel and I were vegetarians for a while in UK in 1997/98, because of watching animal cruelty programs. These images and the associated propaganda made eating bacon and chicken unpalatable. In Australia, for a few different reasons I was a vegetarian, and at one point a vegan. This vegetarian experience resulted from potential side effects of prophylactic drug treatment. When I acquired latent tuberculosis in Alice Springs, the medication caused a metallic taste sensation when I ate meat, yeast or drank alcohol, so I had to abstain from all three. In 2011 in Tasmania, I was diagnosed with degenerative bone disease. As I tried to improve my fitness to combat the effects of the disease, I relinquished all animal products for a short period and became vegan. However, I struggled without eggs in my diet and eventually I became a vegetarian again. My friends in Hobart, who have only ever known me as a vegan or vegetarian will find it hard to believe that I later stooped to a level of carnivorous depravity.

Arriving in France, a country that is renowned for its cuisine, and in particular the variety of meat dishes, we struggled from the start. Even at motorway service areas or in restaurants, we found it hard to find nutritionally sustaining vegetarian food. In the supermarkets, the meat is a lot cheaper than soya protein or meat replacements and, unless in season, vegetables are not cheap either. Luckily, arriving in September the glut of seasonal produce means lower prices and we survive on roasted vegetables, stews and ratatouille. One evening Julia and Phil, a local expat couple who had been in France for over eight years, invite us to dinner. They own and run a successful dairy farm and are big meat eaters. Knowing that we are vegetarian Julia makes a delicious pumpkin soup starter and vegetable curry for the main course. We talk about French food traditions and local community events like the meal following the 'chasse', a French hunting event, that all revolve around food. Julia tells us that many French people struggle to entertain vegetarians, and that it could preclude us from wedding invitations or attending community events like a hog-roast.

As December approaches, we are already encountering financial difficulties. The cost of putting food on our plates has become more of an issue. Not wanting to put us in the position of being perceived as needing charity, Julia offers us a frozen shoulder of wild boar from the 'chasse'. Although her family are big meat eaters, they are not big fans of wild boar. On a sunny, yet cold, December afternoon, we debate the issue of our possible dietary conversion over a cup of tea in the garden, at great length. The reasons why we do not eat meat, possible reasons why we should, and more importantly how fussy can we afford to be right now? The newly acquired slab of meat is defrosting as we ponder making a decision out of desperation rather than principle. Cooking and eating this piece of wild pig is as far away from our current diet as you can possible get. I have to admit that for me, making the transition from vegetarian to a meat eater is harder than it is from meat eater to vegetarian.

The defrosted meat looks dark like game and Julia has warned us that it will need to marinate as it can have a harsh flavour. The following day Nigel logs onto the internet outside the cafe in Chabanais and looks up marinade recipes. He searches for a cheap marinade to make from existing store cupboard items. There is a choice of recipes, but to fit our minimal store cupboard selection he takes some ingredients from three different recipes and comes up with our frugal in France marinade. He carefully prepares the mixture:

Wild Boar Marinade

Two glasses of red wine.
An egg-cup full of cider vinegar.
Three cloves of garlic chopped.
One large onion quartered.
Four cloves.
Two bay leaves.
A sprig of fresh oregano.
Season with black pepper and sea salt.

Put all the ingredients into a pan and bring to the boil, simmering for five minutes. Allow to cool before pouring over the wild boar joint. Marinade for a one to two days turning and basting every few hours.

Nigel unwraps and washes the meat, before pouring over the marinade mixture. He then covers the meat in aluminium foil and leaves it overnight. He decides that one night is enough time as he is suddenly eager to cook and eat this meat. I think he is hungry today. Still not sure that I can or will eat it, we slowly cook it on top of the wood burner. Nigel tends his meat creation with care, basting it and turning it as we discuss the meaty aroma that now fills the one small room we occupy in our little cottage. The smells wafting through the house are reminiscent of a Sunday roast when the children were small, and we cooked in the Aga. The Sunday joint of meat would be the centrepiece to our large Sunday gathering of all seven children on a good weekend (all ex partners willing). I miss those days.

Right, let's get back to the wild boar. After a day of cooking, the meat is finally ready and plated up to rest. Nigel is eager to sample it, which surprises me, as despite his hunger I doubted his ability to eat meat again. However, as he tussles to control his mood when hungry, and he is struggling on our reduced rations of late, he gallantly offers to take the first bite. He loves it. He is back in the land of carnivores. Jaime has always been a meat lover and only ever a reluctant vegetarian by default, when no meat was allowed in the house. She is next in line for the wild boar tasting. She loves it too. Now it is my turn. The dark meat now looks even more like game but smells like beef. I take my wafer thin slice and eat it. I am not sure if I was expecting a sudden epiphany of food appreciation, but it does nothing for me. It is not that I dislike it, but it does not excite my palate initially. I know that finding a source of protein is one of our biggest challenges. It is free food, and if we can eat this, then the cheap dietary range of meat at the supermarkets will expand our affordable menu.

Nigel makes a roast dinner, and we manage to make the wild boar joint last for three nights as our main meal. There is also enough for us to have slices of it cold in a baguette for lunch on two of the days. Protein overload after a recent financially induced food drought, feels gluttonous, but my stomach welcomes it. So the transition is made; we buy cheap chicken for less than three euros, and make one chicken last for two days between three of us. Then we make soup with the carcass. It is now cheaper to eat meat than vegetables - fact.

With meat back on the menu and our pride in relation to accepting any freebies on the back burner, the next big hurdle is to get used to plucking and drawing pheasants. Julia's neighbour, who uses their land to shoot pheasants, often takes her one or two as a thank you gesture. She is too polite to say that they are not keen on them. Now that we have made the conversion to meat eaters Julia offers them to us, glad that we appreciate them and that she does not need to persuade Phil and Andrew to eat them. The first time we collect a pheasant from her we decide that if we are all going to eat it, then we all have to play a part in the preparation. The pheasant has been hanging at Julia's for two days and so is ready for preparation and eating. We hang the bird by its feet, which are tied with blue string, on a long rusty nail outside near the bread oven, and gingerly start plucking it. Jaime does not like this, especially as every time we pull at the now stone cold bird, feathers fly and blood drips from its beak. Nigel rolls his eyes as the blood splashes onto his freshly applied wall covering on the bread oven, and the feathers begin to stick to the blood splashes.

I am a born and bred country girl. As a child, my mum brought up three children while working multiple jobs, so we often accompanied her to work in the school holidays. In the run up to Christmas that meant turkey and cockerel plucking at the local farm. I remember standing for hours on end in a shed, quarter filled with pure white feathers, in a haze of dust. The sound of slaughter from behind the screen at the end of the shed filled the air. The birds, freshly killed, came out on the zip wire hanging by their trussed feet. Most had their heads in place and necks broken but, on a bad day, some would circle the shed with their heads missing from an overzealous slaughterman. Therefore, I am not at a total novice to this business of plucking and gutting the birds, but we are talking about repeating activities from many decades ago, so can I really do this now?

The answer is yes. As you will find out in the next chapter, the animal rearing, slaughtering and butchering continues with birds of various breeds, now that we are honing our craft. Well, I am honing the craft. Jaime and Nigel are reluctant participants in the preparation, but are first in line for the meals that I produce.

CHAPTER 8 MY GARDEN AND OTHER ANIMALS

From Glass Half Full: Our Australian Adventure

The 'boys' came out of the warehouse in their sky crates precariously high on a forklift truck. With their black noses pushed against the metal grids of the sky crates, they looked so small and vulnerable. The French workers looked quite bemused as we quickly got them out of the sky crates and hugged them.

With the fears for our boys in transit now allayed, relief was finally experienced. However, the word relief seems like an understatement for the level of apprehension and anxiety experienced. The act of waiting for our precious cargo to arrive from Australia was nerve racking. We act as if we are expectant parents eager for our new arrivals. As we wait we ponder whether Dave and Buster will settle into French life, and in particular, how will they adapt to the French climate. We are fortunate to arrive from Tasmania and not Queensland or Alice Springs, where the temperature change would have been harsher.

We need not have worried. The dogs take over the cave in the house to start with, sniffing out age-old animal dust and digging into the trodden earth floor. I half expect bones to be dug up.

Occasionally, well almost every night, Nigel brings them upstairs to sleep, providing us with extra warmth through their body heat during the night. Nigel feels sorry for them sleeping in the cold, damp cave downstairs. In late October, they progress to sleeping in the barn in their sky crates, and spending their days in a fenced area of the garden. By the spring, the boys have upgraded into purpose built kennels. He makes the kennels using wooden pallets from Nigel and Ginny's alpaca farm where Jaime helps with the feeding and general alpaca care. Insulated and felted, their accommodation has a better roof on it than parts of our house. Our boys remain local celebrities, as they are unusual looking dogs in rural France. People stop and ask what breed they are, and enquire about their breeding background when we are out walking. Our French neighbours are still bemused at dogs herding cattle instead of sheep!

Our first summer in France fulfils my dream, once lost in Australia, of living my version of 'The Good Life', an amazing high point for me. Since 2011, when floods and circumstances led to us leaving our woodland home in Millmerran, Queensland, I have missed our self-sufficient lifestyle. I enjoyed growing the vegetables for our daily needs and tending our chickens. Now I get a chance to resurrect that dream and keep our French freezer full. Here in France we start our crops early in February. We enjoy an array of crop successes all through the summer. Our final harvest is our pumpkins, in October. We grow onions and garlic, which are enormous, strong and tasty. Our harvest of two massive crops of new potatoes after planting in March and July is the talk of the French gardeners and Yvette brings her family and friends to look at them each week.

When I harvest the first crop, I give her a small basket of potatoes, which brings tears to her eyes, and then mine. We have enjoyed our home-grown new potatoes out of season, and with our Christmas dinner. From May onwards, we do not buy any vegetables from the supermarket or markets, and the freezer is filling nicely. I am happy to be achieving my goal. That said this achievement has not been without its challenges. These came in the form of pests, extended dry periods, and garden flooding. Despite these challenges, we held firm to the goal and my garden and our animals are the centre of my Good Life.

July starts with 33-degree heat and continues sitting between 25-30 degrees throughout the month. Our dry, parched vegetable garden is manually watered each morning and evening with thirteen watering cans of water. My cheap plastic watering can from Super U holds eleven litres of water each time, which we draw from the brook at the bottom of the garden. This physically hard, but necessary task means life or death, success or failure to my vegetable growing mission.

Another of our favourite pastimes this summer is foraging for wild food, fruits and nuts. We make nettle tea, which eases the symptoms of asthma and hay fever. We forage for chestnuts, which we roast and eat as snacks, make into stuffing balls and freeze for our Christmas dinner and then we pickle the remainder. Blackberry season sees my expanding number of jam jars joining the array of pickles in my pantry and the elderberries make a delightful fruity cordial. Nigel makes some homemade cider from windfall apples and marrow rum from our enormous overgrown courgettes. As we settle into winter, it is reassuring to see our cupboards full of home produced pickles, jams, preserves and home-grown vegetables in the freezer. Our pumpkins, onions, garlic and potatoes are all stored in a cool, dry area of the barn.

As part of our good life experience, we indulge our love of micro-smallholding. Our attempt this time involves keeping some chickens and ducks for eggs, and breeding, I have to say now, after a year of trying it, I wonder if I am cut out for this. As much as I love the idea of it, and paddling around in mud in my wellington boots is awesome, there are two main problems. Firstly, I panic far too much, about the animals we keep. Secondly, I sometimes become too attached. Now, my family will say the second point is a lie, due to my transition from vegan to butcher in less than sixteen months. This year has seen me dispatch, pluck and butcher two cockerels, one chicken and two ducks. What have I become?

Not all has run smoothly in relation to our animal keeping escapades. I think it is the time to tell the chicken story. When we first arrive, we agree that once the dog enclosure is up, and veggie patch allocated, we must find room to keep some chickens. We want to be self-sufficient in our egg supply. As point of lay hens are too expensive for our frugal budget, we decide to take a long tail approach and get chicks. Short-term pain for long-term gains, so they say. We find a woman that is selling two week old chicks at the local Sunday vide grenier (flea market) in Confolens. It is a rainy day, but despite this we walk past her many times too afraid to ask the questions like, are they female, how old are they and how much do they cost? Eventually, Jaime and Nigel coerce me into approaching the woman, and we buy five, two-week-old chicks all supposed females, for ten euros.

Two Dogs and a Suitcase

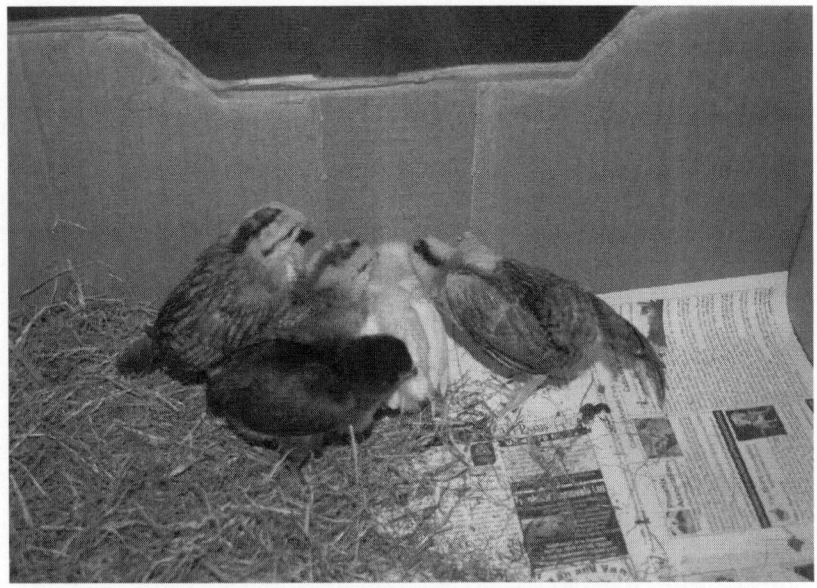

They are due to be point of lay by July and so in an unusual move in most people eyes and, as a temporary measure, we plan to keep them in Jaime's bedroom with her rabbit, of which more later. Their housing consists of a variety of boxes and barricaded areas until Nigel constructs a chicken house, and they are big enough to live outdoors. We nickname them the Spice Girls. The small, pale chick is Baby Spice. The larger, black chick is Scary Spice. The ginger chick is of course going to be Ginger Spice. The white, regal looking chick, with a longer than normal neck is Posh Spice and the other ordinary looking one is Sporty Spice by default.

Once outside they grow quite at a rapid rate. However, Ginger Spice is the first to make a noise, which at first sounds like a chicken under attack. It soon turns into a proper cock-a-doodle-do. I have read on the internet that they can imitate other birds, and several cockerels crow near to our house, so I hope this is the case. However, Ginger is not alone in developing this male characteristic and as his morning crowing matures the others start to either copy him or join in. That is ok if they copy, we think to ourselves, and with one male maybe, we can breed them. Then Scary Spice, now towering over the other birds, starts on cue each morning. Her size and clumsiness earns her the new nickname of Miranda, after Miranda Hart the larger than life comedian in the BBC television comedy series 'Miranda.' The pattern continues, with no eggs produced by any of the so-called hens.

By July instead of five laying hens, we have four confirmed cockerels and one hen, Baby Spice. She starts producing her one egg a day as expected. Obviously, we cannot keep four cockerels, so I dispatch Sporty, and we eat him. Next is Miranda, who puts up a fight, hurts my wrist and tastes horrible.

Therefore, when it is Ginger's turn, we take him for a ride in the car and release him down a country lane, so at least the foxes will have a good meal. That leaves Baby and Posh Spice. That is ok, I think to myself, a breeding pair. That is until Posh starts getting quite aggressive when we enter the enclosure. Thinking he is guarding his chick, pardon the pun, we try not to intervene, but as the bullying behaviour increases towards Baby Spice Nigel finds it hard to ignore. One evening Nigel comes home from work and is relaxing by pottering around in the garden with the animals. I am inside preparing dinner.

"I have dispatched Posh," he says entering the kitchen.

"What? Did you let it go?" I say this because Nigel has never killed anything; he even rescues spiders. His only participation, to date, has been to hold the doomed birds in pillowcases, so that he could not see their eyes, whilst I break their necks.

"No, I killed it."

"Get out of here, you haven't."

"I have."

"Where is it? How did you do it?"

"It's on the floor in the barn, it wouldn't stop flapping."

"Are you sure it's dead?"

"I don't know, that's your department."

We both go the barn and view the disarray caused by blood and feathers, in my newly created utility area. Posh is indeed dead, so I hang him up. I still find Nigel's actions difficult to comprehend as I recount this story, as it is so out of character for him.

After the chicken purchasing and cockerel issues, we decide to try duck breeding and rearing for eggs and meat. The priority in setting out on this mission is to buy from an English-speaking person. Therefore, we search and find a local English expat duck breeder, as we want to make sure we get two males and two females as breeding pairs.

We find and buy two black males and what we believe to be two white female Muscovy ducks. Nigel adjusts the entrance to the chicken coop to ensure that they can enter at night, and for shelter when needed. In planning for breeding, we utilise a large shed and secure run obtained in a typically good life Tom and Barbara style barter. We exchange our grass cutting labour for the shed, in these frugal times. However, as the ducks mature one remains small whilst the others grew at a much faster rate. After scouring the internet, I resort to purchasing a second hand copy of 'Storeys Guide to Raising Ducks' for £1.87 on eBay. It helps me identify that we have one female and three males, aids my diagnosis of the wet feather issue and gives me the knowledge for the dispatching of the now unnecessary males. One black male takes a fancy to my small white female duck. He begins jumping on her back continuously throughout the day, for some love action. So much so, that she develops chronic wet feather syndrome. We have to take what we now know to be the female duck out and let her live in the barn. As much as I wanted to breed them, I could not bear seeing my female duck treated like that. Sorry ducks, a life of abstinence for you I am afraid, hence why two of them end up on the dinner table over Christmas 2013; but that is another story.

Panic and irrational behaviour demonstrate itself one morning when I go into the barn to get the wood in for the day and feed the female duck. Notice I did not name them this time; anyway with my jobs done I secure the door and leave. An hour later, I go to check and see if she has laid her egg. Her food is uneaten, and I cannot find her. I check all the possible escape routes, and all my defences are intact. As we are building the master bedroom and my office in the mezzanine of the barn, I have to assume she has somehow flown up a level and is now in the roof space. Nigel is away in the UK, running in the Para's 10 TAB (Tactical Advance to Battle) in Colchester. This is a 16 km cross-country endurance race in which the entrants wear a Bergen, or rucksack, filled to weigh 35 lb or 16 kg. Being alone in the house, I am forbidden to climb the aging oak ladder we found in the barn on our arrival. Therefore, I secure the barn and leave pondering some David Blaine style illusions of disappearing birds and rabbits. However, there is no sign of a struggle, and despite the gaping hole in the roof, I feel confident no predator has been and taken her away for a hearty meal.

Later, when I next go to collect wood from the barn, I search around again this time with the torch. There is no noise or movement, so despite her being AWOL I get the watering can and start to refill her bucket. Suddenly she appears from behind some old French doors given to us by Tim from a restaurant renovation. She is eager for a drink. I remain puzzled until I look behind the doors and discovered a nest made of sticks, concrete dust and old paper. In the centre is an egg. Now I know it is not fertilised, but I do not have the heart to take it from her so for today at least she keeps it. I mark it with my garden pen, so we know it is an old egg, because when my egg-eating husband returns he will not be happy that I am wasting eggs. However, for now, she can brood and at least she is alive and safe. I felt upset at the thought of losing her, even temporarily.

I should also add that in the duck enclosure there is also Jaime's dwarf white rabbit.

Rosie the rabbit

Our neighbours have been eyeing up this pet rabbit, which has been resident in the garden enclosure since Jaime left for the UK in June. Whenever Yvette comes to review my garden she looks at Rosie the rabbit, which turns out to be more of a Robert, and says, "mange?" and rubs her tummy.

"Non, Non!" I say, unable to remember the word for pet, despite the fact that I keep looking it up and then forgetting it again. We gain great kudos from our elderly French neighbours when we start dispatching our chickens and ducks; it does not make sense to them keeping animals that are not for eating. So, back to Rosie. When we bought her from a St Junien pet shop we asked for a female rabbit, well at least I thought we did. I remember the shop assistant picking up the rabbit and after turning it to inspect its rear end saying, "Oui," meaning yes. For several months, Rosie has lived with Jaime in her bedroom. Jaime would trim its nails with her nail clippers and apart from chewing the cable to the Wii and eating the Christmas tree, Rosie has been no trouble.

One day Jaime came downstairs holding Rosie, which is unusual, since the rabbit is never allowed downstairs, as it is not secure. She could slip outside where the boys would not hesitate to eat her.

"Rosie has cancer," Jaime splutters with tear-filled eyes. I look at her with a mix of annoyance at the interruption, and surprise at the use of the word cancer.

"What on earth are you talking about?"

"She has lumps."

"Let me see," I say impatiently as I stop writing and take Rosie from her. I turn the rabbit upside down on my lap and roll my eyes. As soon as I see the lumps, I realise what the issue is.

"Jaime," I say, closing my eyes in that way that I hate when people do it to me. It is as if they are reading the inside of their eyelids. "You remember that talk we had many years ago about the birds and bees?"

"Oh, mum…. stop it; not that, not now, this is serious."

"I know."

A silence descends whilst we both stare at the lumps. Rosie tries to release herself/himself from my grasp.

"Well Rosie is a boy. It's not cancer, those lumps are his testicles."

"Eww! Mum don't talk like that, it's disgusting. She can't be, can she?"

With that, we seek internet confirmation. After seeing the very clear photographs on Google, Jaime is at last convinced. I thought Jaime would be relieved that it is not cancer, but it turns out that her main concern is that we cannot change her/his name now because he/she responds to being called Rosie.

I should also include in my tales of other animals, my attempt at keeping cats, to deal with our mouse problem. Our rustic lifestyle in rural France, in a house with more holes than a leaky bucket, also means that mice are an issue. Brazen little blighters they are too. They run across the floor in front of me without fear, and they tip toe over the slipper on my feet whilst I sit writing at the table. It has to stop; what if they start dancing around when we have guests, not that we have many guests, but you get the point. One day Julia comes round for coffee, and a mouse starts popping out from under the cooker. Luckily, Julia lives on a farm and is used to such things, but it still does not sit well with me. Therefore, the answer is a cat.

Now the boys will not like us having a cat, but the boys are not keeping the mice away, so there is no alternative. In August we start searching for cats being given away on the Expat forums and find two that are free to a good home from a couple who are returning to live in the UK. The cats are two years old, good mousers and are up to date with vaccinations, which is perfect. They already have names, Stinky and Maccy;

Stinky

Maccy

I do not know if I want to stand in the garden calling those names, particularly 'Stinky,' but the cats are probably too old for us to change them. We collect them, bring them home and keep them indoors, with some difficulty, for few days. As they are older cats and used to being outside, they are keen to go and explore, although Stinky is quite timid at first and sleeps for long periods. We let Maccy, the more adventurous one of them out first. He runs away. However, the following night Nigel runs downstairs just before midnight as he hears some kind of commotion going on in the garden. The boys are 'intruder barking' and jumping up at the fence. Nigel goes to investigate, and as he shines the torch around the perimeter, he sees Maccy cornered by Dave. He grabs Maccy from inside the dog's enclosure, sustaining multiple scratches in the process. After throwing him indoors, he returns to check Dave for scratch wounds. Cats can cause terrible wounds to dogs, especially if they scratch their nose area. Luckily, both Dave and Maccy have only minor wounds. The next day Maccy slips out and I never see him again. Great. We keep the other one in for a while longer. He is more cautious when he ventures outside for the first time, returning to the sanctuary of the barn when the boys bark at him. Within ten days, both of my cats are missing in action. Although disappointed, I am grateful I have not found them run over on the road. We decide that the problem could have been that they were older, and so after a rethink we decide that a kitten is the way to go.

After I return from my visit to the UK in September, for Jaime's birthday, we start searching for a kitten. We see a five-week-old abandoned kitten advertised on Facebook and arrange to collect him on Sunday 22nd September. Hazel, the woman who found him and advertised him, agrees to drive half way, as they are located three hours' drive away. We meet her at Melle, a pretty market town in the Deux-Sèvres department, an hour and half's drive from Chirac.

The kitten fits neatly in the palm of Nigel's hand and for someone who does not like cats, Nigel is the biggest softy with George. It is always a democratic affair when we choose the names for our pets. It involves writing down names and either putting them is a hat, or just debating them. Nigel and I start this process when we get home, but as I am considering the names of our boys, Dave and Buster, I write down the name George, no particular reason it just seems to fit. Without further discussion, I name him George.

We go from 'no cats in the bedroom' to George sleeping on one of my cardigans on our bed each night. Nigel worries that he will squash him when he rolls over in the night as if it is a baby. In the morning playtime takes place on the bed, whilst we have a cup of tea. Then mouse-catching training continues downstairs while we eat breakfast and watch the BBC news.

Apparently, the throwing and catching of a furry mouse is training and not play. He is still small and at four months of age, I did not want to let him outside in case he ran away too. The mice have departed since George's arrival, even though he has not caught any of them indoors. We have achieved the mission to be mice free, but George has totally taken over the house and our lives. He sleeps around my neck as I write, and he seeks attention by scratching his face against Nigel's stubbly chin when he gets home from work.

A few months later and George has become a hardened mouse catcher, displaying his gifts each morning by the door. The thought of what he has played with, or eaten, means that his rubbing against Nigel's chin is unpleasant. His latest trick is letting himself into the food cupboard in the kitchen if we make him wait too long for his dried cat biscuits. Who would have foreseen this happening in a household previously smitten by dogs.

CHAPTER 9 FRIENDS, NEIGHBOURS AND OTHER PEOPLE

Our move to rural France from Australia came with certain expectations. For one, we expected to be able to submerge ourselves into French culture, community and lifestyle, living amongst principally French neighbours by picking a rural location. This expectation did not come to fruition because most of the people we meet in the village are British. Although Chirac has a population of around seven hundred people, it has a higher than average percentage of resident British and Australian expats. I am not entirely sure why that is the case, and we have not met them all yet. Maybe this quiet village location appealed to them for the same reasons it did to us. It is near to good road and rail links which makes visiting the UK easy and affordable. It has major cities forty minutes in either direction, yet the house prices are lower than average.

Dean and Veena live near the village school, they are an expat couple who are also friends of Julia. We met Dean one day in the street outside our house. He was walking around with his mobile in his hand looking like he was trying to pick up a network connection. We greet him with "Bonjour" as he passes, but he recognises we are English and responds with, "Hello." After Jaime's return, she was introduced to Veena, a fellow horse lover with two horses. Veena let Jaime ride one of her horses in the run up to leaving for her horse grooming apprenticeship. Jaime enjoyed spending time with their two girls, Megan and Kara. Even though they were a lot younger than her, it gave her a chance to get out of the house and socialise.

Tim and Nicky become good friends to Nigel and me. As well as being a work colleague, Tim has also helped Nigel with a few car issues during our time in France. Nicky and I refer to them as the 'Two Victors,' after the moaning character of Victor Meldrew in the BBC TV show 'One Foot in the Grave'. They both have a tendency to act like grumpy old men, moaning about insignificant things. Nicky and I joke about it a lot. However, where cars are concerned, Tim is your man. On one such occasion when we needed to replace the Peugeot, but now with a substantially reduced budget, Nigel finds a van for sale in France. Originally, a UK import, it is now French registered. Owned by a retired UK builder it has regularly been in use for 25 years. It has a very long wheelbase, which makes it an excellent choice for transporting renovation materials like beams and plasterboard. As I do not drive anymore, and the van needs to be collected from a small village over an hour's drive away Nigel takes the Peugeot. He parks it in a small village car park near to the church where he picks up the van. Tim and Nigel plan to go and collect the Peugeot after work one evening in coming week. Nigel drives the van home, and although it needs some cosmetic work, it drives well. Nigel and Tim do bits and pieces to it and make plans to fix the exhaust, which is noisy. Work becomes busy, and they still have not found the time to go and collect the Peugeot. One evening Julia messages me to say that there is an angry sounding post on the AngloINFO forum to say a UK car has been abandoned outside someone's house and that it has been reported to the Gendarmes. Julia, thinking the registration number is familiar, wonders if it is ours. I was not sure because I could not remember the registration of the car or the name of the village where Nigel left it. The next day I tell Nigel.

"For goodness sake it's in the middle of nowhere, there is plenty of parking for everyone and it's not abandoned." He pauses for a moment before saying, "It had to be British people complaining, not the French. British people in France are all so precious about parking in exactly the same place. And God forbid that anything that might be an eyesore and devalue their property." He is annoyed now.

Tim and Nigel make plans to go and collect the Peugeot and Nigel messages the person on AngloINFO to let them know that it is awaiting collection by a scrap dealer, to avoid any confrontation when they arrive. As it has been a few weeks the road tax has run out, the faulty handbrake has seized, and the back tyre, which we pump up daily, is flat. When Nigel and Tim arrive to collect it, they are ready with their story about being scrap dealers, as the curtains of the houses nearby start twitching. With Tim's truck in place, they position the ramps so that they can drive straight onto the truck. It is a steep incline; this will cause scraping on the concrete, so Tim, an ex-banger racer and more experienced than Nigel at this manoeuvre, drives it on. Tim cannot help but sound the horn and wave at the curtain twitchers as they drive away, just to have the last word. No one had the nerve to come out and say anything to them, or even ask any questions.

The house next to us, as you walk towards the church, is a holiday home owned by a delightful English couple called Keith and Maria. They have a gorgeous chocolate Labrador called Holly, who they bring with them when they come on holiday. Next door to Keith and Maria is another English couple, who became permanent residents in France on their retirement. Next door to them is a strange man, who we will call Mr Q. I cannot write the name that Nigel calls Mr Q in private, as some would call it offensive. Nigel gave him a potentially offensive nickname after an encounter in the street a few months ago. One evening after work, Nigel leaves to walk the boys. As he turns the corner of a small lane opposite the house, Mr Q is walking towards him. Nigel still has a lot to do after walking the boys, and after a hard day at work, all he wants is to eat his dinner to sit and enjoy a glass of wine.

Therefore, he can be tetchy when something or someone holds him up. In addition to which Mr Q approaches too fast and too close for Dave and Busters liking. They begin barking and snapping at him. Mr Q fails to acknowledge the potential threat to him from the boys and ends up at a lead length away from Nigel, who is annoyed at having to pull the boys in hard to stop them from snapping his now articulating arms.

"Do you mind if I ask you a personal question?" Mr Q says without any form of polite greeting to acknowledge the start of a conversation.

Nigel does not enjoy small talk, and he dislikes it even more with relative strangers. If it is also of a personal nature this puts his patience to the test. Therefore, this opening gambit from Mr Q means Nigel is up for giving him a piece of his mind.

"Try me," he says relishing where this conversation will go next.

"Do you believe in God?"

"That is personal, what's it got to do with you?"

"Well something is going to happen to you," he said.

"Are you for real?" Nigel says now staring him straight in the eye, "the only thing that's going to happen to me is that I am walking away from you. Weirdo!"

"Oh, I didn't mean to offend you," he said.

"I am not offended. I do not talk about sex, politics or religion with people I do not know, okay. Now I suggest you stay away from me."

"It's just that I am a Scientologist and …"

Nigel interrupts him. "You can stop right there. If I want someone to preach Scientology to me, I will go and visit Tom Cruise. Now get out of my way and don't ever speak to or even look at me, or my family, again."

Mr Q never spoke to Nigel again, and he crosses the road when passing our house. I think he got the message. I digress.

You walk a fine line when you meet people of your own ethnicity in a foreign country, as to whether you befriend them or not. It can come across as an obligation that you should because of the 'we Brits stick together' mentality. The other question is whether you allow yourself the luxury of choosing your friends based on mutual interests as you would in the UK or Australia. If we are honest, we do not all go round and start knocking on the doors of our neighbours when we move within other countries. However, it seems in France you are rude if you do not do that within the expat community. We have never liked living in the pockets of our neighbours, in whatever country we have lived. So once again I suppose we come across as snobs, wanting to choose who we will, or will not, befriend. Oh well.

Many people dream of a life living in the French countryside, a new life in a new country. Hang on a minute, I have written those words before. Oh yes, we have done this before. Am I a gypsy? It is a dream location and meeting UK expats, explaining that we are originally from the UK but that we have arrived here via Australia, often raises eyebrows. The most common reaction from people, who will end up not being our friends, is:

"That's crazy why would you leave Australia for France?"

Or

"I would give an arm and a leg for the chance to live in Australia. You must be mad."

"We have moved here from Australia." Those few words signify that only something of deep significance would invoke such a dramatic change. Some more receptive, dare I say intelligent people wait to gauge our reaction and our body language as we speak. These people have become our friends in France. These friends we feel safe to share the joys and challenges of our Australian adventure with face to face. We somehow sense that they may, on some level, relate or empathise with our need to live nearer to the children. We encounter many scathing comments like, 'Well you shouldn't have left your kids in the first place' and 'What a waste of money.' Words are cheap, but if they loiter in your subconscious uninvited, they still eat away at you. In my opinion, the four and half years we spent in Australia can never be considered a waste of time, energy, resources or emotion. It is a time in our lives, which changed some of our family relationships in profound ways. I will never regret it, and a little piece of my adventurous spirit will always remain in Australia. As I write this, two of my children, Samantha and Jaime want to, or are returning to, live in Australia. The timeframe for their moves is unknown, so who knows what the future will hold?

First impressions count, and I decide after a few of these encounters that if people want to know the real story they can wait and buy the book. 'Glass Half Full, Our Australian Adventure' is one of my works in progress. I do not need sympathy or charity; I make my own way in this world, now and always. I do not need anyone's approval for this hair-brained scheme on which we are embarking. The reality is that we had no idea; we were clueless when we arrived about how hard this would be. We have been naive and in some respects foolish, despite our extensive research, but you only learn by experience and mistakes. It is going to be one crazy experience even by our standards. We are in France on a bucket list mission, and that is the way we describe how we came to be there to would be doubters. Early on we learn that not everyone is worthy of the time it takes to relate our story. My problem is that to tell half the story feels deceitful if I do not trust them enough to tell them the real reasons we left Australia. In doing so, I did not give them the opportunity to know us for who we are. I decide that if I need to share my story with honesty I should do in a way that I feel comfortable with, and that is by writing about it. I prepare articles for the expat publications Etcetera magazine and Deux Sevres, which gives a synopsis of how we ended up in France.

Anyway, back to France. Apart from the British people already resident in the village of Chirac, others drift into our radar. We receive an amazing response to my articles in the form of emails, telephone calls and visits. Some people want to see our renovation project, and share tips from their experiences. Others are inquisitive about Dave and Buster, who are now local celebrities. Some are fellow writers; it appears rural France attracts and inspires many in the writing fraternity. They are not all British expats. We meet people from America, Australia, New Zealand and Germany. The news of our arrival filters through the expat grapevine at speed.

Our French neighbour Yvette is a widow with a large extended family that visits her each week on different days. The family all arrive on Sundays at her house, once the village cafeteria that she owned and operated for many years. A babbling brook, as the estate agent described it, runs along the bottom of the both Yvette's and our garden. Over the long, hot summer, I loved to go and sit, dangling my feet in the icy cold water at the end of the day, especially after a day of hard work on the house or garden. I sometimes wonder why my French neighbours stand with their arms folded across their chests looking at me. Never saying anything, just watching whilst I paddle. 'Crazy English woman' is more than likely what they think. One day, I tell an Australian expat friend about my evening pastime. About how the neighbours watch me but say nothing. She tells me that the neighbour's husband died in the brook. The story goes that he took his own life, after having a stroke, not wanting to be a burden on this family. Nobody goes in the brook or draws water from it now; well at least they didn't until I arrived. Imagine my horror when I recall the previous evening when I had even taken a glass of red wine with me to sit and soak my feet. When I next saw Yvette, I could not look at her, after disrespecting her husband's memory. I do not paddle in the brook anymore.

Our other neighbours who live opposite are Andre and Janine. They have lived in Chirac for over sixty years. Andre worked as the village blacksmith for fifty of those years and his house and garden demonstrate the craft he perfected, with his wrought iron railings, crafted iron features adorning the sheds, archways and garden planters.

CHAPTER 10 FRUGALLY DOES IT

As we settle into 2013 in France, I do not have any practical way of earning money. Nigel is insistent that I continue writing 'Glass Half Full', and that I can pay him later for the privilege. Therefore, my contribution to our financial well-being is keeping us fed, which includes growing as much produce as possible, whilst trying to keep some chickens and later ducks for eggs and meat. Then using those ingredients I make cheap cost effective meals. At least, it sounds that straightforward on paper. As you have read, the animal side of this has not run smoothly, so I am optimistic for my vegetables. This challenge from Nigel inspires the inner chef in me. As Rob will tell you, cooking has never been one of my best skills. In the days of my single parenthood when Samantha and Rob were young, they were at times undiplomatic about my cookery skills. They were also uncomplimentary of my culinary prowess after a night shift at the nursing home when I had not been to the supermarket. One day instead of Rob's favourite sausage and baked beans, I made fish sticks with white cannellini beans, not quite the same in eyes of a six-year-old boy. It is funny because Rob and now Nigel compare my cooking to that of Susan, in the BBC television comedy 'My Family' starring Robert Lindsay. Zoe Wanamaker plays Susan, wife, mother and tour guide who despite being an awful cook does not let it hinder her culinary style. She regularly improvises when she does not have the correct ingredients. The most memorable episode for me is Susan's attempt at cooking duck à l'orange with no oranges. In the show, the family often secretly hide or dispose of her food offerings without her noticing.

Frugally does it is how I approach this lean period in our current adventure. The word frugal allegedly originates from the Latin word frugalis or frugi meaning cheap or thrifty. The dictionary definitions focus on implying that one is careful or saving by being sparing in the use of money, food or resources. In frugal times, we need to employ frugal measures. After two attempts at growing tomatoes, this summer, the tomato crops end up suffering from tomato blight. This is despite Andre and Janine giving me some of their tomato plants as a helping hand. The two rows, each three-foot high, of tomato plants situated near the wall of the barn form a hedge like formation. They receive a mix of sun and shade, the ideal growing conditions. I first notice our tomato plants turning black on the stems, as the green tomatoes weigh heavy on the vines waiting to ripen. As these plants are my first early crop, I assume that an overnight frost or a sudden drop in temperature has damaged them. Unsure what to do I make a judgement call and decide to watch and wait to see if the tomatoes will still ripen. They did not, and soon dark spots consume the green tomatoes; infected and useless, they cannot even be disposed of in my compost bin. Undeterred I try again with a combination of my own and Andre's tomato plants. On this second planting, I again spot the signs early while there is an abundance of green tomatoes still on the plants. I cannot risk wasting any more tomatoes, after all the time and physical effort that goes into growing and keeping them watered. I research whether it is safe to eat or use the green tomatoes from plants that may have the blight. It appears that if I take them off before the vine becomes infected then they are good to use. That means I need to harvest now. I end up with ten kilograms of green tomatoes that are now sitting in the barn on a wooden pallet, as I contemplate how to use them. I know you can eat green tomatoes raw like red ones. We ate them in Australia when we lived in the woods, but somehow after seeing the effect of the tomato-blight, they are not appealing to my taste buds. Therefore, I research on the internet what else I can do with them. With my modest, somewhat frugal store cupboard, the cheapest option is to make green tomato chutney. I find a recipe and true to my improvisation reputation; I adapt it.

SJ's Green Tomato Chutney
Recipe
1 lb brown onions (I used home-grown leeks instead)
2 kg green tomatoes chopped
½ tsp salt
1-tsp pickling spice (instead, I used curry powder!)
1-pint brown vinegar
1 lb pickling sugar (I used granulated)

Method
Cook the onion in a little water until soft. Add the chopped tomatoes, salt, curry powder and cook until tender. Add the vinegar and sugar; simmer to reduce to a jam like consistency. Remove from the heat and store in sterilised jars. This chutney will keep for twelve months in cool conditions.

With ten kilograms of tomatoes I make five batches. In total, I end up with thirty jars, of all shapes and sizes, of my curried green tomato chutney, which is delicious. We have eaten it with bread and cheese at home and on picnics with cold meats. It has been an accompaniment to my duck curry made with Christmas meal leftovers. The warming effect as the slight kick of the curry powder hits the back of your throat is incredible. I also add two tablespoons full to stews and casseroles. To my surprise, this is popular, even with the children, who do not like the look of the green substance in the jars.

When money is tight, and you have a hard working renovation man in the house, some form of fast acting energy food is essential. The physical effort involved in the work in and around the house and garden intensifies over the summer months. After too many episodes of Nigel's hunger causing him to break something, or get frustrated with inanimate objects, we are in dire need of a solution. I have never enjoyed baking, a throwback to my home economics teacher in my teenage years. However, I know I need to be able to make something quick and tasty from our meagre basic ingredients. I am not saying that Nigel is fussy, but he knows what he likes. I find a scone recipe, for which I do not have the correct ingredients, so I renamed them:

Chirac cheesy scones.
Recipe
2 cups of self-raising flour
50 g of cold butter (or hard margarine if you are looking to reduce costs.)
1 tsp baking powder (I did not use this.)
½ cup of grated cheese (an ideal use for stale hard cheese.)
½ tsp mustard
½ tsp salt
¼-pint milk
1 egg (from our one laying chicken.) Later I make these with a duck egg and the rich yellow yoke enhances the flavour and texture of the scones.
Freshly chopped mixed herbs and grated garlic.

Method
Sieve the flour, salt and baking powder into a bowl; rub in the cold butter with your fingertips, as they are the coldest part of your hands. Add the mustard to the milk beat the egg in a bowl then add to the mustard milk mixture. Add the grated cheese to the flour mix and slowly add the milk liquid until it makes a firm dough ball. Do not knead or handle it too much. Divide it into ten balls and place them on a well-greased baking tray. Lightly press the top of each ball to flatten the top and place some grated cheese on the top. Bake for 12-15 minutes in a hot oven on the middle shelf. The extra grated cheese on the top makes a crunchy golden topping.

When you feel like you are permanently cooking on a budget your menu can become a little dull. Although we have never been big eaters of takeaway food, we do enjoy a good pizza. However, we both dislike the thick, doughy crust that some take away pizzas give you. In our local supermarket, a large frozen pizza costs around five euros. They look like cardboard placemats, with food leftovers on them, as there is minimal, unappetising topping. I decide to be inventive and using my newly acquired bread making skills, I decide to try a Jamie Oliver Italian pizza dough recipe. Even though I change the ingredients, I do try to adhere to his method. Sorry, Jamie Oliver.

Italian pizza dough
Recipe
1 kg Italian tipo flour (I used French basic plain flour)
1 tsp salt
2 x 7g yeast sachets
1 tsp sugar
4 tbsp olive oil
650 ml of warm water.

Method
Sieve the flour and salt onto a clean surface. With the back of a tablespoon, make a well in the centre. In a jug mix the yeast, sugar and olive oil into the warm water and let it rest for five minutes. Slowly, a little at a time pour the liquid mixture into the well and with a fork gently mix it in. As the dough starts to come together form it into a ball, and work it with your hands on a floured surface. Knead for a few minutes until the dough is springy. Place it in a floured bowl with a damp tea towel on the top. Then put it in a warm place or outside in the sun until the dough ball has doubled in size. This takes approximately 40 minutes. Remove the dough ball and knock back the dough by kneading the air out, which takes approximately five minutes. The dough is then ready to use or can put in the fridge in cling wrap to use later. Each batch makes 6-8 medium size pizza bases so when there are only the three of us I roll them out and freeze them.

When it comes to the toppings, my creative cooking skills go into overdrive. On weeks when we cannot afford meat, especially over the summer when fresh vegetables are available in the garden, our toppings include leek, spinach and green beans. I use my green tomato chutney instead of tomato paste to coat the pizza base. Our home-grown leeks are so tasty that I plait up my onions and garlic bulbs for use over the winter, and we use the leeks as an onion alternative, for mince recipes and making gravy. In Australia zucchini, or courgettes as they referred to in Europe, are eaten roasted, barbecued or in stir-fries. They harvest them while they are still small to retain their flavour. When we planted six courgette plants at the end of the garden, near the brook, Yvette shook her head. She made big arm movements indicating huge growth. I assumed that she meant the foliage, as I know they produce large leaves like pumpkins, which is why we planted them together. My thinking was that the foliage from both sets of plants would cover the ugly spots where the outhouse had been.

As the courgettes start to form, we pick them off at the size we are familiar with in Australia. The more we pick them, the more they grow. Each morning new ones appear. Then one weekend whilst picking and weeding I come across a huge marrows.

How had we missed these developing courgettes that has now mutated into marrows weighing almost five kilograms? I am not a huge fan of marrow despite loving the taste of courgette, so I research an easy way to use this unexpected harvest. I find a recipe for courgette cake, which I thought would make a change from the many vegetable savoury dishes I am creating. As supply is outstripping demand in the vegetable department and the freezer is filling, I do not want to waste anything.

Courgette cake
Recipe
60 g raisins
250 g grated courgette
2 eggs
125 ml olive oil
150 g sugar
225 g plain flour
½ tsp bicarbonate of soda
½ tsp baking powder (which I still do not have.)

Method
Soak the raisins in some warm water for 20 minutes to soften them. Put the grated courgette into a colander placed over a bowl. Press down with a wooden spoon and let the juice drain for 30 minutes before use.

Sieve the flour into a bowl; add the sugar and bicarbonate of soda. (I always worry using bicarbonate of soda in recipes. Especially because the only reason I have any in the house is for cleaning the glass door of my wood burner.) Fold in the grated courgette then drain and add the raisins. Beat the eggs and fold in with a spatula while stirring add the olive oil. Pour the mixture into a greased baking tin and cook for approximately thirty minutes on medium heat.

As the summer progresses and the number of courgettes spirals out of control, I make batches of the cake for the freezer. When Nigel becomes bored of it, I pimp up the recipe by adding grated chillies and dark chocolate, which is awesome. Cake alone does not control the monsters I create at the bottom of the garden, and so my recipe for curried courgette chutney is born. This in addition to courgette soup finally helps me to get them under control. Just when I thought some vegetable respite is in sight the pumpkins are ready.

The spiralling branches of the pumpkin plants wind their way over and through the cloche, over the brook along the bank and around the tree stumps. The pumpkins as they first formed resemble Chinese paper lanterns. However, from July to October they go into overdrive and expand like water-filled balloons. The weight of the pumpkins leads to them hanging precariously close to the water in the brook. Soon they become too heavy for me to move them to attend my other plants. When we harvest them between late September and mid-October, in time for Halloween, we end up with twenty-two pumpkins in storage. The six largest I make into pumpkin pie filling, soups and use for mash instead of potatoes with our meals.

Once the hen and the duck start to lay eggs, I steer us away from baguettes and bread for lunches. I opt instead for open-faced omelettes, and quiches, as this gives me the opportunity to use up leftover courgette slices, sliced green tomatoes, radish and leeks. I thought I would never finish with the radishes. Initially, it was lovely having them washed, chilled and sliced with a salad, but as the weather got hotter, they grew faster and became hotter tasting. Even Nigel struggled with them in his lunch box on workdays. I didn't even know if you could make a chutney or relish, as it turned out, from radishes.

With no real recipe, I based the ingredients on a pickle or chutney:

Radish Relish
Recipe
2 cups of diced radishes
2 cups of diced leeks
1 large onion chopped fine
1 tsp salt
1 cup sugar
1 tbsp mustard
2 tsp coriander
1 cup brown vinegar

Method

I used my favourite cooking method for this experiment. Put all the ingredients in the pan, boil it, taste and bottle it when thickened.

Over glasses of wine and evenings tasting my variations on a theme utilising pumpkins, courgettes, leeks, green beans and other vegetables, I decide to start writing my frugal cookbook. After a lot of debate and playing with words and phrases I finally decide on a title which says exactly what it is and what it offers. 'Our Frugal summer in Charente: An Expat's Kitchen Garden Journal' is due for publication later in the summer to help provide some inspiration to gardeners with excess harvest time produce. Some of the cookbook recipes you can look forward to include:

Chestnut - nut roast and chestnut stuffing: Our successful foraging expedition in the local lanes and playing fields delivered three sacks of chestnuts.

Pumpkin curry, tarts, casseroles and my favourite pumpkin dumplings. I became addicted to these much to the detriment of my waistline.

Luxury fish pie made from fish scraps from the fish counter.

Fig biscuits from a bucketful of free figs from the garden of renovation project Tim and Nigel worked on.

Jam steamed pudding and variations thereof made with my variety of homemade jams. All made with foraged and free fruits such a damsons, apples, plums and greengages.

Nigel's contribution to the cookbook is his recipes for his home brew. These include cider, marrow rum, and elderberry wine and cordial.

CHAPTER 11 HOBART TO LE HAVRE

Part of our preparations to move from Hobart to Chirac included deciding what to keep. The items we chose to keep would be sent by sea freight. In hindsight, and as ever shining a positive light on this process, we were lucky we did not own many belongings, or so we thought. It is surprising how quickly the boxes fill with just clothes, shoes and my precious books from charity shops.

"You paid cents for those, is it worth paying hundreds of dollars to take them to France?" Nigel said, on more than one occasion as we packed, repacked and divided our belongings into piles of 'to go,' 'to donate to charity' or 'to sell.'

"I am not losing my books again, where I go they go."

I started my book collection again for the first time after the floods, and there would be no more starting again for my collection, or me.

By the time we had finished, there were thirty boxes and one bicycle box left at John's house for collection by the courier company. As promised, two days after our departure the boxes were collected. They were then taken to the Hobart depot for weighing and documenting ready for movement to Melbourne before heading off by sea to France. We arranged for the boxes to travel overland on arrival in France to Lyon our nearest pick up point, four hours from our house. The estimated timeframe for arrival in France was three to four months from leaving Melbourne. As they left Hobart at the end of September, that meant they left Melbourne in early October. Therefore, arrival in France was expected in January 2013. Apart from receiving the invoice to pay once they had been weighed there was nothing else for us to do until January 2013, or so we thought. On 27th November, during our regular Tuesday email checking session at McDonalds, St. Junien, I receive an email from a French freight agent in Le Havre. In their best-typed English the message, which looks and reads as if it has been copied and pasted from Google translate without even adding my name, says:

"Dear,

To delivered your cargo in our warehouse of Lyon CFS you have to: Paid the arrival charges for an amount of 441.48 euros in cash or by swift bank. Custom cleared your goods by a forwarding agent as: Miro: 02.35.51.81.81. Only before the customs clearing of your shipment and only after the payment of arrival charges we will deliver your cargo to our Lyon warehouse. Kindly note than you have only 7 days of free time since the unstuffing days in our warehouse in Le Havre to paid and customs cleared your goods. After the 7 days of free time some, storage charges will be bill to you. Cordialement / Best Regards"

I go outside and try to call the logistics office. I need to find out when the seven days started and how to pay the fees, but my mobile credit ran out mid enquiry. I emailed back.

"I am sorry we got disconnected on the telephone.

To confirm what I need to know is:

1. Have the boxes arrived at Le Havre and if so when did the 7 days start?

2. I will need to pay by bank transfer, as I cannot get to Le Havre to pay cash,

Can you email me the details?

3. How will I know when I can collect from Lyon, can I receive a telephone call as I do not have daily access to email?"

In response almost immediately, I receive this, bearing in mind it is Tuesday 27th:

"The cargo still unstuffed since 25/11. So you have until Friday included to come in Le Havre to paid us, and customs cleared your goods before storage charges."

Frustration and panic have now set in, so we decide to call in reinforcements in the form of Julia and Phil. We organise to go to their farm the following morning. Our plan is that Phil will call the logistics office, speak to them in French, ask our questions and help us organise the transfer to Lyon. Julia, as always the perfect host, makes cups of coffee as Phil calls and establishes the facts. The boxes arrived on Sunday, and we need to collect them by Friday. If we cannot go to Le Havre and visit Customs to process the documentation then they cannot transfer them to Lyon as planned. This was not part of the plan. Over more coffee, we send emails to try to get quotes to hire a van. After unsuccessful emails and telephone calls due to the short notice of the booking, we face facts. We will need to drive to Le Havre, clear customs ourselves and bring the boxes back in our car, a Peugeot 406 estate, currently with a fuel blockage issue and no breakdown cover.

Le Havre port, the second largest in France, is also France's largest container port. The name Le Havre literally translates as 'the harbour' or 'the port.' This major French city is approximately 50 km west of Rouen on the shore of the Channel. It has great road links to Paris and throughout France due to its port status and importance. A search on Google maps finds that it is a five and half hour drive from Chirac, and is estimated to cost approximately fifty euros in fuel each way. In addition, it will cost approximately forty euros in tolls. The toll roads are great, less traffic and easy driving. They are easy to use as you can pay in cash or by card. The only difference for those of us with right hand drive cars is that the passenger has to deal with the payment through their window.

We need to be at the logistics office by ten o'clock on Friday. Here we pick up the documentation we need to go to the customs office, and then to the freight warehouse. We compile the documentation needed; passports, driving licences and proof of house ownership in France. Nigel strips away anything not permanently attached to the inside of the car to create more storage space. Headrests, seats, tools, nothing is sacred. The reliability of the car is a big worry, and we decide to distract ourselves from the 'what if' scenarios by throwing ourselves into some extreme physical labour. We decide to lay the concrete floors in the cave. We only talk about positive things when we work on the house to give it good karma. Therefore, instead of discussing the car and the boxes we talk about the upcoming visits from the children, which is exciting and upbeat. We have a cement mixer on loan from Tim, and Nigel has the bags of cement and a pile of ballast in the barn. We shovel, mix and carry more buckets full of cement than I care to remember. Nigel levels it and we stand, admiring the wet, shiny pool that will be our kitchen floor base with a sense of achievement.

Our plan is set; Jaime will go and stay with Julia on the Thursday night so that we can leave in the early hours of Friday morning, enabling us to be in Le Havre early for the first part of the bureaucratic exercise. We make enough sandwiches; flasks and snack food to last for the marathon estimated twelve-hour return journey. The boys will have to stay in the cave, and Julia and Jaime will visit to feed and walk them during the afternoon. As we get into the shell of the car, in the darkness of the early hours, it feels to me as if we are going on an adventure. Nigel, however, is too consumed with worry for such fanciful thoughts. We will be heading north towards Paris travelling through, or past, Poitiers, Tours, Le Mans and Alençon.

Within a few kilometres, the car is coughing and spluttering. Nigel then notices that our headlights are now without their legally required deflectors. As we make our first stop, we establish that the brake lights are also stuck on. We have no choice; we must get to Le Havre, and so it is carry on regardless. Cars are flashing at us because our lights appear to be on full beam, we pray for daylight to come so we can turn the lights off. Despite this, we arrive at the logistics office as scheduled just before ten o'clock. As we enter, not knowing who to see or where to go, it is like being a contestant in the game show, Treasure Hunt. I imagine Anneka Rice, in her tight fitting tracksuit, racing around looking for clues in our emails and the signage. I should add here that I do not resemble Anneka Rice in any way, and I do not wear tight fitting fluorescent tracksuits. After attempting to seek help from a woman in a small office on the ground floor, who ignores us, we spot the logo of the logistics company. We follow the images up the staircase. In the office on the top floor a young man, trying hard to speak English, checks our passports, takes our money and issues a receipt. He gives us a map to our next checkpoint, the customs office in the centre of Le Havre.

We race down the stairs, get into the car and the GPS takes us in circles as we enter numerous one-way systems. We spot the customs office, and need to find somewhere to park quickly. Time is ticking, and it is almost eleven o'clock as we enter the office. Inside, as we approach the desk, two large women look up at us. One of them peers over her glasses, but neither attempt to stand and come to the desk to greet us.

"Bonjour: Hello." I say quite loudly by my standards.

I can feel the other people waiting are now staring, at me, as it is obvious I am not French. The women look at one another and the younger of the two gets up and come to the counter. I hand over the logistics paperwork and our passports, etc., and watch as she flicks through the pieces of paper. She takes them to her colleague, who starts to tap the keyboard. The scene unfolds resembling a sketch from the British television comedy show 'Little Britain'. The woman tapping the keyboard shakes her head in that familiar way that indicates something is not right. What is going on? I am tired and getting frustrated now.

"Parlez-vous Anglais?"

"Un petit peu." Oh, my god, how many times have I heard these words now, knowing it means nil?

"Is there a problem?" I say completely forgetting about trying to speak French.

"These goods, your personal objects?" says the younger woman.

"Yes. Oui."

"Non furniture? You have an inventory?"

"Non. No we don't, it was not required in Australia as they are personal effects only."

"So it's not for you to sell here in France?"

"Non." I say in French to ensure she understands. As if any of our belongings would have any value to French people.

"Can you prove you are permanent resident in France?"

I show her the contract of sale for the house.

"Non." she replies.

"What do you need as proof?"

"I need certificate of permanent residence from the Maire of your commune."

Nigel and I look at each other, and realise we are both thinking the same thing; 'No one mentioned this, and we are not doing this journey again.'

"We were not told we needed this is. Is there any other way of doing this?"

Another lengthy silence ensues as I study the clock on the wall above their heads. I focus in on the ticking as the time edges closer to the twelve noon compulsory shut down. We still have to get to the freight warehouse before noon.

As if sensing my irritation, which is bordering on anger, she stamps the form and gives me a card with her email address on.

"You must email me the permanent residency declaration from the Maire within seven days. If you do not you will receive a 'facture,' invoice for the tax due on imported items."

I am not interested in any of this; we have what we need to go the next, and hopefully final, checkpoint in this bureaucratic game. We race back to the car and program in the address of the warehouse, which is apparently fifteen minutes away. Once out of the city centre we are on a long straight dual carriageway, which has traffic lights at every junction to a port gate. We catch every set on red. It is silent in the car as if this will make the time go slower, or the traffic lights turn green faster. We arrive at the warehouse at ten minutes to twelve. Okay we can do this, I approach the reception protected by a cigarette stained glass window, which is firmly closed. I tap on the glass in the absence of a bell or buzzer and a woman with thin-pursed lips approaches already scowling at me. I give her the documentation and my passport. Behind me, the warehousemen are parking up their forklifts in preparation for their lunch break. The woman takes my passport, documents, and closes the window. Do I stay here or go somewhere else? She sits back at her desk, so I tap the window again to find out what is happening. She points to a man walking towards a forklift and then returns to the paperwork on her desk. I stay at the window, and she eventually gets up and opens it again. I point to my passport on her desk and she says "non" in a stern, quite scary tone, and closes the window.

I am so angry, tired and frustrated and I can feel the tears welling up in my eyes, but I will not cry in front of her. I go outside to tell Nigel what has happened and see that a forklift is placing a euro-sized pallet behind our car. The total weight of our belongings is half a ton, in old money, 500 kg in metric terms. This sounds massive, but seeing it on one pallet made the sum total of our possessions look quite small. It is the equivalent of five 100 kg men, as Nigel so eloquently said as we stand discussing the total weight of the car for the return journey. Is the positioning of the full pallet intentional so that we are not able to move the car without emptying the pallet? At exactly twelve noon, the forklift reverses away, and the metal shutters come crashing down.

"Let's get this unloaded, and then we will deal with your passport." Nigel says.

The pallet and our boxes are tightly wrapped in polythene. It is obvious that damage has occurred to some of the boxes as cardboard edges are protruding. They are stretching the polythene forming shapes like limbs resembling a scene from one of the Alien movies. At the office window, I can see maybe ten members of office staff and warehousemen, pointing and laughing. They obviously do not think we can get thirty-one boxes weighing, half a tonne into our car. We will show them; they do not know that one of

Nigel's nicknames is Mr Packer. He can pack any car with shopping, camping gear; you name it, better than anyone I have ever known. We even moved house once in Ford Fiesta! Nigel removes the plastic wrapping from the boxes and begins to load the inside of the car. The car is soon full, but there are still boxes on the pallet. We work in silence, passing items back and forth to each other. He loads the bike box, which is flat, onto the roof to use as a base for a makeshift roof rack. On top of that, he adds more layers of boxes.

When Nigel finally says, "that's it for the roof," we both stare at the pallet. There are four boxes remaining.

"Right, we have to empty the boxes and fill in the gaps." My eyes are scanning the car, but there are no obvious gaps to be seen.

Nigel notices my now caffeine depleted facial expression.

"Fill the door pockets, foot wells, anywhere, and then you can have coffee."

The magic words; I am now in the zone to pack this beast of a workhorse, which is just a family estate car, to the brink. I fill the glove box, spaces under both our seats, the empty lunchboxes. These last few boxes contain tools, books and clothes. I begin stuffing and pushing things with little care as if I am competing in the 1970's British game show, 'The Generation Game.'

After thirty minutes, the car is packed, and the pallet is empty. Nigel picks it up and tosses it on the grass verge. He even manages to stuff the raggedy polythene packaging into the car so as not leave any litter.

"Right, go and knock on the door and ask for your passport."

"Oh please come with me, she's a witch,"

"Are you for real, get on with it woman?"

"Ok then," I grumble to myself as I stomp off feeling somewhat annoyed.

I knock on the door; no one answers. I look over at Nigel, hoping he will come and rescue me, but he just shouts, "Knock harder."

I knock again loudly, still nothing. Then I notice another door, not the one I used before, so I go and knock on that. As I knock, it opens. I step inside. Ah ha. I am in the inner sanctum; a step closer to my passport. I see the glass window and walk towards it. Behind the glass, the warehousemen and office workers are eating from a table laid out like a buffet with salad, meat and cheeses. There are two bottles of red wine open and in full flow. I tap the window, hoping and praying someone other than the witch woman will come, but no she looks up at me and then looks away. I am annoyed now so I knock again. This time I point to my passport, which is beside her plate on her desk, but it is now sporting a blob of her beetroot vinegar. She picks up my passport, wipes it on her skirt, opens the window and hands it to me. The window closes with the glass shuddering, but with no words spoken. I walk away in disgust.

Once outside I get in the car and Nigel says, "What happened?"

"Let's go get some coffee. I want to go home."

After a brief stop for some hot coffee, as our flasks are empty, we start the long slow drive home, fully loaded. The extra weight is straining the already sick car, but we plod on. About half way home the steering wheel starts shaking. Nigel makes several stops to examine the car, but nothing is obviously wrong, so we keep going.

"That's it, it is too dangerous. Something is going to fall off. We need to get some help." Nigel says as we approach the two hours from home marker.

We pull into the emergency layby, near to the orange coloured emergency telephone. Luckily for us these emergency phones are located every couple of kilometres. We have passed quite a few concerned where the next one might be. Nigel puts the hazard lights on, and begins searching for the red emergency triangle. He soon realises that the compulsory red triangle, which needs to be placed thirty metres behind the vehicle, is buried beneath the boxes.

"Oh great!" echoes from the back of the car.

We both get out and go the telephone because we know they will be speaking in French. It will need a combined effort to make the operator understand our predicament. We endeavour to say that we are on the A 10 heading towards Poitiers. We think that she says okay she will send someone well at least that is what we hope, as we hang up on the call. Within minutes, a patrol vehicle pulls up, and the patrol officer who gets out speaks no English. He gestures to Nigel to put his high visibility vest on, which luckily is not buried under the boxes. He goes with Nigel, looks at the steering wheel, and then kicks at the front wheels. Then after some pointing at the boxes, he makes the international hand sign for telephone. He puts his left hand into a makeshift telephone using his thumb and little finger. We think he is asking, 'have we called for help.' After making a call on his mobile, which we assume is checking that we have requested some help he leaves.

Stranded. So near, yet so far. I call Julia to let her know there is a slight problem, trying to put some positive spin on our situation. All is well at the house with the dogs, and she says she will take Jaime back to the farm until she hears from us. Dusk is descending as, thirty-five minutes later, the tow truck arrives. A dark haired man jumps out leaving another man in the cab. He speaks a little English straight away, obviously seeing the UK registration plate. He says he will load the car and take us, and the car, to his garage. The euro signs are popping out of our eyeballs at the thought of the costs involved in this latest hiccup, but we have no choice. I am told to get my bag and get in the truck. I climb into the back of the double cab, and Nigel gets in beside me. My body language must be so transparent because he puts one arm around me and his other hand on my right knee.

"Don't worry, it'll be okay," he says.

When the driver returns a few minutes later the truck moves off into the traffic, but within a few metres, we are slowing down again. I look at Nigel, as there is no exit from the main road coming up, just fields. We are sitting in the back like naughty kids in the car, not daring to speak or move. As the truck slows to a halt, the driver gets out and opens the gate, which leads to a small track. I am scared now; this is like a bad dream or a scene from a horror movie. I know I am a drama queen with an imagination to match, but how do we know this is the recovery truck sent to get us. It could be an opportunist kidnapper of British people stranded in France. Why are we driving into a track? Why does he get out and shut the gate behind the truck? The tow truck driver and the other man in the front of the cab continue talking French. We try to peer out of the windows into the enveloping darkness to see where they are taking us. Suddenly the track merges with the road and we are in what looks like a small town. On the left, we pull into the garage, and I feel as if I can breathe again. The driver gets out and opens the cab door for us. He calls over a young boy, who could be his apprentice or his son, and they examine the car.

It is dark now, and they are looking at the wheels with torches and pushing at the car. As if it is going to shake with all that weight in there. Gesturing for me to go and wait inside, he takes Nigel and the car for a test drive. I stand in the garage, which looks like it is ready for closing. Why does everywhere close today when we go in? They are gone for what seems like a long time, but is about fifteen minutes.

"The wheels didn't wobble one bit," Nigel says as he gets out of the car.

"Well that's good isn't it?" I say

"No, I look like an idiot."

The mechanic explains that the problem is probably the wheel hub joint, which is deteriorating quickly with the amount of weight on board. He takes us through to his office and in his broken, but most welcome English explains that the car is ok to continue driving. He says that the weight is not helping the cars performance, so 'go slow' is his advice. He reaches for his invoice pad, and I know I am holding my breath again. He scribbles away in French and then turns the piece of paper around and underlines the total. One hundred and forty-eight euros, thank God, that could have been a lot worse. We pay, say our goodbyes and navigate our way back to the A 10. I call Julia, who agrees to take Jaime home, and we settle in for the slowest drive back to our little house.

Two Dogs and a Suitcase

Fully loaded and squeezed into the barn!

It is almost nine o'clock by the time we get home. Jaime, Julia and her son Andrew are upstairs in our cold living room. They have tried unsuccessfully to light our wood burner and are sitting with their jackets on. Exhausted we plan to catch up the next day. With no thoughts of unloading the car tonight, we manage to park the car in the barn. After all, that car and those boxes really are all our possessions.

The following day we are all excited to get the boxes into the house. As the house is in part a building site and we are living on the landing, we agree to open and unpack just the things we need. However, once we start looking inside, it is like Christmas as we start opening boxes and spreading the contents across the floor. Within minutes my books are out and piling up against the wall. Jaime has CD's and ornaments that are spreading out across the floor. When Nigel sees what is happening he orders us to stop. That is until I notice that behind him is an array of tools in my bedroom. We compromise on unpacking the kitchen items and a few personal items that will resist the impact of the renovation dirt and dust, packing the remainder back into the boxes. These boxes now become the equivalent of Lego as we build our own furniture with them.

CHAPTER 12 CHRISTMAS IN FRANCE

"Don't wait for the perfect moment. Take a moment and make it perfect"

I do not know where this quote originated, but I need this mental kick up the backside right now. The stress of the first few months in France, in relation to Jaime, has taken its toll on our relationship. In addition, my writing and our enthusiasm for our project have added to my perceived worries. Nigel has been unable to find work and the remaining money from the house purchase is quickly diminishing. Even in the weeks when we have not bought renovation materials, the day-to-day expenditure eats away at our bank balance. Everything is hard and time intensive, as we have no mod cons like a washing machine, bathroom or central heating. As I write, I hear hypocritical negativity oozing from every word. How can I say these things when I am the one who advocates positivity to my family, friends and those in need of motivation? Where can I find my positivity when everything seems so hopeless yet again?

The prospect that one of us will need to work away from home in UK looms ever closer. In an act of pure selfishness, I do not want to give up my writing. However, as my bone health worsens in the colder climate I also wonder if I am physically fit enough to return to hands-on nursing. On the other hand, if Nigel goes, can I manage the physical work here to keep the house going? The daily chores include cutting wood, walking the dogs, carrying water buckets and collecting starter sticks. The list is seemly endless. Everything is physical, even cooking a meal in our makeshift kitchen in the corner of our bedroom. I uncharacteristically let myself drift into an almost depressed state. I find myself not getting out of bed when the church bells ring at eight in the morning. Instead, I cover myself over and drift in and out of slumber. What is there to get up for? Jaime is hibernating in her room, unhappy at being in France and having no friends or social life. Nigel is irritable with Jaime and now today, for the first time in a long time, he is irritable with me. As the sunlight enters the bedroom through the half-open shutters, I roll over and discover Nigel is still in bed. He has not bothered to get up either today, which it is unlike him.

"Are you having a lay in my sweetheart?" I sense he is awake even with his back to me.

"Well, if you're not getting up, why should I bother," he says, as I roll over to cuddle up to him. Then the pep talk begins. I listen as he lectures me, like one of the children. I immediately and instinctively resent it, but deep down I know everything he says is true.

"You have given up Sarah." He never calls me Sarah at home, it is always sweetheart. That cuts me to the core, and hurts more than any other words said to me. Am I giving up? If I have given up, then there is no hope for anyone else. I am the glue that holds this family together in tough times, and this is definitely a tough time. So what do I do in this tough time? I take to my bed and sulk at our misfortune. It is not misfortune; if we are honest, it is self-inflicted naive behaviour. To coin a phrase we are Clueless in Charente. We fell in love with the idea of a new life in France and despite everything that is happening I love being here. However, the practicalities are extreme for a family with no French language skills. We cannot even go and seek help at the equivalent to the social security office.

After my lecture, I decide to stop wallowing in self-pity and start a list of ideas to troubleshoot our current issues. A new day and a new positive start. Ironically today, the 21st December 2012, is the day when the Mayan Mexican people predict the world is going to end. Just in case it is true Samantha texts me from Australia to say, 'In case the world ends today, I love you Mum.' This makes me smile. I text back to her, 'The end of the world can wait, I am not finished yet.' Just texting these positive sounding words means I am back in control. Mrs Positivity has regained her focus and says bring it on world. It is as if my renewed positive frame of mind is a gift from above because things start happening.

Jaime gets a call from the equitation centre in Suffolk, about her application to become an apprentice horse groom. They want to conduct a telephone interview and this alone puts a smile on her face and by default on Nigel's too. She is so excited at the challenge of leaving home and starting a career. If the interview is successful, there is a potential downside. She will need return flights to the UK, accommodation and coach travel. I had better watch out, if I dwell on this expenditure, my positive flame might extinguish again, so I get back to focusing on our income. After lengthy discussions, we decide it is more practical for Nigel to go to the UK to find work. I would need to transfer my nursing registration from Tasmania back to UK before I could work as a Registered General Nurse, whereas Nigel can go and find courier work, driving and labouring jobs whilst he transfers his security licence. In addition, because I am still not driving, it would be more difficult for me to live and work there and get back to France on days off for visits. Therefore, with the decision made, job hunting on our trips to find Wi-Fi outside the school in Chabanais begins in earnest. I start the administrative tasks; he will need a bank account, flight and coach ticket.

As we are also in the run up to Christmas, my recent self-pitying behaviour has put a dampener on making Christmas preparations. Therefore Jaime and I decide we will make some Christmas decorations. Even though we have no spare money for luxuries we decide to indulge in some Christmas spirit. We take a trip to the Christmas market in Chassenon on the Saturday before Christmas. After over ten days of rain, today is sunny, despite being extremely cold. However, this combination is Christmassy, a feeling we missed whilst living in Australia. It is a typically French affair with stalls set out in barns with straw on the floor. Meats of all descriptions, roasted and cured. There are cheeses, sausages, cakes and food of all varieties from local artisans for sale. A choir of carol singers serenade the Christmas shoppers. They sing French and English versions of Christmas carols. There is a sense of peace that descends. Despite the busy market, as we walk through past the church, it casts its comforting shadow over the proceedings.

Our Christmas

When you have a child in the house of whatever age, if it is Christmas then you have to stick to certain family traditions. I am not referring to gifts and presents, I mean more the tree, some form of decorations and a Christmas meal. We decide to buy a small chicken to roast for our Christmas meal. Jaime helps me to make some mince pies and Nigel is in charge of the roast potatoes. We know that due to Jaime's depressed state of mind it is vital that some degree of Christmas normality exists. Despite the pressures we are under, we decide to make every effort for Jaime. Jaime has no close friends. Her mental shutdown and emotional distance from Nigel means I am the only person providing any meaningful physical contact. She needs something to love, and we find the ideal gift, a dwarf rabbit. As we will not travel to St Junien, any more before Christmas we have to buy it today. We ask for a female rabbit, as males have a reputation for aggression. We buy it and take it home in a cardboard box.

This spontaneous decision means we are not prepared at home for a new addition. However, given the state of the house Jaime can keep a rabbit in her bedroom and let it run free in her room. With the wood flooring, this will be fine until spring when Nigel will build a hutch. When we get home, Jaime has completed her Christmas task of decorating individual placemats that we found amongst our belongings from Tasmania. They do not match, but we devise a plan for Jaime to decorate them with snippets of tinsel, coloured card and golden letters from Nigel's craft box. We are not supposed to look in there. We will use the placemats for our Christmas meal, on our lap trays to look festive.

Unable to hide the rabbit for four days because the boys already know there is an intruder, we decide it will give Jaime a boost to have an early Christmas gift. Nigel transfers the rabbit into a larger cardboard box with some hay, and hides it up high in the cave. Later that afternoon as we sit down to yet another Christmas movie, Nigel appears with the box. He has made a bow using my sewing ribbon. Nigel hands Jaime the box.

"Father Christmas popped by early for you this year." Jaime looks shocked at Nigel's display of tenderness but takes the box from him. She opens the top, and when she spots the small bundle of white fur, she starts to cry. She is still so of full of pent up emotion that the slightest provocation opens the floodgates. As her tears fall, I know I am crying too. I want to ease her mental anguish so badly. She reaches in and lifts out the rabbit. She cuddles it as it snuggles into her chest; Nigel grabs his camera, and as she looks over her shoulder towards him, our eyes meet.

"Thank you," she says.

"Merry Christmas Sweet pea, what are going to call her?"

"Rosie. Rosie the rabbit, because she's small and pretty like Rob's old girlfriend."

"Ok, well no rush for a name." Nigel says pragmatically, since Rob and Rosie are no longer a couple.

In a recently rare moment of bonding, Nigel and Jaime spend time together building rabbit defences in her bedroom. Rosie can then run free when Jaime is in the room with her. They raise all electric wires in case of chewing, and the main rule is that she must not be allowed to get free. If the boys smell her, they will hunt her down. That night, Jaime went to bed and put Rosie to in her box with hay, food and water. I think she had the most peaceful night's sleep since she came back from the UK. We all need physical contact and closeness. There are times when nurturing and caring for another living creature can help to heal your mental wounds. Rosie is Jaime's medication now and her sense of purpose. Something to get up for in the morning, and someone who needs her attention.

The Christmas period, when you do not have family and friends visiting or work to go to, can be a long haul. With prolonged periods of rain, we are captive in our living area on the landing. We have our two free sofas that Phil helped us find from an advert on the AngloINFO forum. A television that Tim and Nicky gave us which is enormous and so heavy that it sits on three of our full packing boxes which form a makeshift television stand. We watch multiple episodes of Come Dine with Me and Christmas cookery shows, but in the afternoons, we let Jaime choose a film to watch. Our Christmas day is quiet; we have made a stocking for Jaime, which consists of useful gifts like toiletries, socks and slippers. We set a Christmas challenge last week and had five euros each to take to GiFi, a cheap shop in St Junien. The aim was to buy lucky dip gifts to be wrapped and put into a decorated cardboard box. The irony of this game is that we all went to the same shop. We all frequented the one-euro aisle and so consequently, we bought some of the same items. Nevertheless, Jaime enjoyed it.

Nigel cooks our Christmas meal and his final treat for Jaime is a small individual Christmas pudding, which he bought from Petticoat Lane, an English food shop in Chabanais.

He divides it into three spoon size pieces. One each, served with the spray cream, which is part of a family tradition, involving spraying it into Jaime's mouth until her mouth is full. It may sound a bit strange to people who have not experienced a Butfield family Christmas; however, it has been a family favourite that all the children have taken part in over the years! Boxing Day Julia and Phil invite us for drinks and a buffet. Some of their family are over from the UK, and it is a nice break for us from the house, which has become our enclosure of late. It also provides an opportunity for Jaime to socialise with Andrew and the children that are visiting. A degree of normality prevails as we put our worries and concerns on the back burner.

CHAPTER 13 DESPERATE MEASURES

The truth is that there is often no one particular answer to life's challenges, sometimes there is no solution just resolution.

New Year's Day 2013 is day 99 in France, Why am I counting? I sound like the presenter on Big Brother television programme. Initially, I started counting the days since Jaime's departure to live with Jack. Then I numbered them in my diary as part of my writing schedule. Now on a motivational and positive note they are engraved in my heart as I count down the days to family reunions when the children visit us in France, or we go and visit them in the UK. There are many reasons, in my head and my heart, to count the days. However, the one set of days I would prefer not to count, as they are now into single figures, are the days until Nigel leaves for the UK to find work. The weather is an idyllic mix of winter sun and a bracing winter breeze. The heat of the sun feels like the blaze of summer when you manage to avoid the breeze that brushes and reddens our cheeks as we walk off the excess of Christmas, as my mum used to say. There are no excesses to walk off, but we decide to do the traditional New Year's Day walk anyway. We are completely over the Christmas family film fest and need to take full advantage of this glorious weather and our precious remaining time together. So any opportunity to escape is grabbed with both hands and enjoyed.

As we walk the lanes between Chirac and Peyras, we discuss the plans for Nigel's imminent departure on 9th January. His plan is to buy a car or small van to live in and use to find work in the UK. He has a list of budget B&B's and even the local homeless shelters in and around areas where he has applied for jobs. Nigel is pragmatic and in no way fussy, as his objective is clear, he needs to find work to earn money to keep our dream and us alive. Therefore, he has applied for jobs as pizza delivery driver, parking enforcement officer and courier to name but a few. It is so hard to find a job in the UK when you are in France. If you do manage to get to speak to someone, the tendency is to want you to pop in and pick up an application form. Alternatively, they invite you to an immediate interview on Wednesday morning, when it is already Tuesday afternoon. There are family members in the UK that he could visit and stay with short term, but pride prevents that being a consideration at this stage. However, if the plan A does not work, then they may be built into plans B and C. The reality of the situation dawns and clouds this perfect start to 2013.

Day 100 and with only a week to go, the reality of my part in this survival plan hits home. As a drop of icy water lands on my cheek, abruptly waking me from my slumber, images race through my sleep impaired consciousness. Floods, water, photographs floating. All totally irrational, I was not even there when the floods came to our home in Australia. Nevertheless, these are images of my belongings. As consciousness dawns, I realise I am in bed, and the roof is leaking again, as rain lashes against the front of our leaky cottage. It is cold and, despite the rain, the boys need walking. The wood needs to be brought in from the barn for the day and evening's use, and the kindling needs to be cut. Jaime and I, as always, will take our rucksacks and scour the hedgerows for twigs and wood that can be dried out for starter sticks. The enormity of all these tasks now becoming my sole responsibility, on top of the daily running of the house, with no basic amenities like a washing machine or bathroom, weighs heavy on my mind.

I am a strong woman in a variety of ways. I have no qualms about being able to cope with my financially induced separation from Nigel. However, I am struggling with my bone pain in this colder climate. I will not complain as this situation is of my own making. I cannot see a doctor, as we had to cancel our health insurance, so I am surviving on anti-inflammatories and Panadol posted to me from Australia and the UK, by Samantha and Rob. It is cheaper than buying it in France. The postwoman must think I am a junkie. Rob sent me a multipack of glucosamine, and as the parcel was difficult to wrap, he emptied the 1000 tablets into a brown envelope. However, he only wrote my address on the parcel and not my name. It had been delivered to every house from the church down to us before reaching me. With one glance, I recognise the schoolboy writing of my son and I admit to ownership of these unidentifiable pills.

Is this the end of the road?

Failure is not a word we, or I, use, probably because of its negative connotations. That said, as we reach the decision that Nigel would need to return to the UK to find work, the word failure creeps into my sub consciousness. It burrows in like a bed bug and eats away at the fibres of my soul until I admit defeat and acknowledge it is there. The time has come for me to face head on some personal fears.

During my nursing career, there were many occasions, almost daily, and sometimes even hourly, when the direct consequences of my actions could have resulted in death or harm to one of my patients. I mean this in the form of medications or treatments administered, actions taken or omissions during emergencies. These were all literal life or death situations, where the actions I did, or did not take, had a direct impact on another human life. This puts my new fears into context and now, in the non-nursing arena of both my personal, and professional life as an author, when I feel anxious about trying something new in an area that I am less confident in, I force myself to consider these questions. If I get it wrong, what is the worst that can happen? Or can anything I do by mistake be amended or corrected without harm to others? In reality, I develop and grow because of my life experiences being a parent, friend, wife, nurse and now author. It makes me realise that facing my fears is easier than I believed possible. The barriers we construct to halt our dreams and ambitions are of our own creation due to our own self-doubt. Break down these perceived barriers and we can do anything. We are all capable of achieving our dreams in whatever form they may take.

Therefore, my task now is to apply this new angle of positive thinking to handle my fears. One of the major impacts on me of Nigel's imminent departure is the necessity for me to face my fear of driving and traffic. I will need to drive the fifteen minutes to Chabanais at least once a week, or a fortnight if my nerves give out on me, for essential shopping. We do not own a freezer and with only a small bar fridge, topping up on shopping will be unavoidable. Nigel has been taking me out on practice runs in the small lanes that surround our home in Chirac. At times, I feel confident again and then suddenly I look in the rear view mirror and a French vehicle is tailgating me. It is normal here, however, the sight of a car behind me throws me into a state of shock. I am unable to think about what to do. I want to stop, but there is nowhere to stop. I want to get out, but I cannot. I then progress into an autopilot like state whilst shaking from head to foot. The relief when I am able to pull over, or park outside our house, is immense, like the proverbial weight being lifted from my shoulders.

Daily I pray for a miracle, just a small one. I do not pray for great riches or anything for myself, just that Nigel or I can find work and that we can get back on track. I do not mind doing it tough, and I can go without even basic things, but with Jaime back in the house, there are limitations on how low we can go. I come to dread when her period is due for the expense of her sanitary products. How awful does that make me as a mum? My faith, simmering on low heat, is finally restored in the space of a five minute telephone call from Tim, who was mending our roof until we ran short of money. He calls on the 8th January 2013, the day before Nigel is due to fly to the UK, to offer him work three days a week as a labourer. We are saved, for now at least. Tim, without realising, has saved us from separation and defeat. Nigel can stay, for now.

However, little did we know that our elation would be short lived. We head off to use the internet to cancel Nigel's travel arrangements, which are already scheduled. Nigel receives the devastating news that one of his closest friends and colleagues, Brian, whom he worked with at the Wrest Point Casino in Hobart had hung himself. Suicide is such an awful word with so many connotations. What does it mean? Nigel is immediately overcome with shock and grief. The resurrection of grief brought to the surface issues of loss that he is still dealing with since the death of his mother Sheila in 2009. Guilt then consumes him. What kind of friend did not prevent this from happening? Would it have happened if we had stayed in Hobart or even in

Australia? What about his beautiful daughter? Who would look after her now? So many guilt ridden questions, but no answers.

In the days and weeks that follow, Nigel starts work, and we attempt to get back on track financially. The work Nigel does with Tim varies in location and type. Sometimes he works thirty minutes from home on a complete renovation of an old watermill in Rochechouart. Other times he will be working, near to Tim's house in Edon, on a house renovation. Both are large building projects, hence Tim's need for a hard working labourer. All the work involves hard physical labour tasks such as, carrying tiles and buckets of cement up ladders for Tim to use. Whatever the task Nigel loves it because he is always in training for the next of the Paras' 10 events.

However, psychologically the realisation is that you are only as strong as the support you have built in around you. We start looking forward to the upcoming visits and counting the days becomes pleasurable again. A large dose of family time, appreciating and counting our blessings. Samantha and Cam are returning from Australia for a visit before their four year work sponsored visa starts. Rob is visiting our new home for the first time in the New Year and then there is a surprise for Nigel, a visit by Clair and Phil to France in March. A visit from Clair and Phil is just the tonic he needs. I help Clair organise this visit with great difficulty. It is extremely hard to keep anything a secret from Nigel; he uses his private investigator skills in everything he does.

We do most of the arranging by email. I act like a spoilt kid at times to get changes made to the house in readiness for their arrival. For example, we are living on the landing, we cannot accommodate guests until we move our living quarters downstairs. Doing that means we need to fit a door to the areas where the toilet is which currently has only a tarpaulin for privacy. I pester Nigel to make the changes to the layout downstairs. I am sure he thinks I am going into the menopause and nesting or something. However, he goes along with it, reluctantly. I pull friends like Julia, and Nigel and Ginny from the alpaca farm into my web of deceit to keep my secret and help with my plans. I conspire with Tim and Nicky for Nigel to have a few days off; Tim is supposed to say he has a private job to do which does not need two people.

"I've got work tomorrow is that okay?" Nigel says looking pleased with himself. Bugger, Tim, has forgotten, I need to text Nicky, I am thinking to myself.

"No, it's not." This statement, or the way I said it, shocks Nigel. Why would I tell him to turn down work, all we ever do on a Saturday morning is the food shopping. He is looking at me, and I am trying to look at him without letting my face give away the cause of my abrupt response. There are two choices; I either have to attempt to lie to his face, to get away with this, or admit to our cunning plan. Anybody that knows Nigel also knows he is a black and white kind of guy. There is no grey; just yes or no, the word 'maybe' does not exist, and the words 'don't know,' do not constitute an answer. As I wrack my brain for a reason why he cannot work I realise it is futile, but I have one last attempt.

"You have to go to the airport to pick up Nigel and Ginny's daughter; remember?"

"That's not this week, is it?"

"Yes." I had asked Nigel and Ginny to be my backup excuse for getting Nigel to drive to Limoges airport tomorrow.

"Well money is more important, they will have to get someone else."

I pause, and he is now staring at me. In that instant, I know I have been found out.

"What's going on?"

I pause again.

"That's great now Clair is going to hate me." I say admitting defeat. Nigel is looking at me in a state of utter confusion.

"What are you talking about?" He says, as I pause again, still wondering if I can get out of this.

"You have to go and get Clair and Phil from the airport tomorrow."

Silence. Then Nigel's face develops a rarely seen smile.

"Is that true?"

"Yes. It was supposed to be a surprise; I am supposed to make you stand there holding a board for Nigel and Ginny's daughter and then Clair and Phil come out of the arrival doors."

"Oh, I get it now, that's why you got moody when I refused to clean out the car," he pauses. I know he is recollecting my actions over the last couple of weeks. "You, stockpiling food like we are going to hibernate for three months, that's because the kids are coming. Making me fit the toilet door. Oh you..."

I can feel tears welling up on my eyes.

"Thank you." Nigel says as he comes over and hugs me. Then just as suddenly, he releases me. "Oh my god where will they sleep, we don't have...."

"Stop. It's all sorted; I have borrowed a camp bed and spare duvets they are hidden under the bed."

"So it's really happening?"

"Yes it is, but Clair will be so annoyed with me you must not tell her you know."

"Okay, that's a deal."

CHAPTER 14 PLAYING AT BEING A TOURIST

When you become an expat in rural France, as opposed to a visitor, you still need to explore and enjoy your new location. As much as we try to explore through the eyes of French residents, it is hard when you feel and behave like a tourist. When we have guests, they expect to visit picturesque and interesting places. Trust me; you have more friends visiting when you live in France. We start close to home in the market towns in which we do our weekly shopping and buy our building materials.

Confolens:

A riverside town located on the Vienne River, it is the point where the Charente and Limousin regions meet. I believe that is why some places use the term Charente Limousine. The town of Confolens is believed to have originated from a township built surrounding a fortress around the eleventh century. There are remains, which make excellent photographic opportunities, of its medieval past. These take the form of bridges, stone walls and houses and other buildings. Today, the numbers of British and expats of other nationalities owning properties and businesses here is increasing due to its location and recently improved travel infrastructure. We like Confolens and often go there for coffee by the river. Sometimes we walk through the tiny streets that weave their way through the town and around the market area. We enjoy walking these streets and reading the historical interest signs.

La Vienne

On my birthday in May 2013 Nigel and Jaime, arrange a picnic by the Vienne River. The views are spectacular. The grey stone walls and the lush green riverbanks are set against the clear blue skies. I like to sit and imagine what life would have been like in medieval times, with horse drawn carriages in the streets and boats on the river. Another favourite place for us in Confolens is the reclamation yard, which is run by a British expat. There is plenty to explore. The rooms and outbuildings are full of building materials; old sinks, doors, windows, beams and baths entice renovators. Anything, removed during a property clearance for demolition, from crockery to tools for the garden is in here. As we aim to restore as many elements of our cottage as possible, being able to source genuine oak beams and various fixtures and fittings is ideal.

Chabanais:

In the Charente is our nearest market town. The scenic views of the Vienne River running through it are a favourite with tourists. In addition to the weekly market held on a Thursday on the banks of the Vienne, there is a range of shops, restaurants, cafes and bars. However, they do not detract from the quiet charm of this small town. Its location and good transport infrastructure make it an excellent venue for sporting events. It provides a range of facilities and open sporting areas for tennis and football. These areas also host local shows such as the circus, vide greniers, fetes and motorcycle rallies. Again, like Confolens, it has some amazing architecture. These features tempt photographers to stroll through the small streets, maybe stopping for coffee on the way. Whenever any of the children come to France, we visit Cafe Clemence for coffee. To be able to sit in the sunshine chatting and enjoying the surroundings is one of the reasons we fell in love with this area. We also, when work permits, attend the monthly expat quiz nights there with Steve and Jackie, another couple we met through my article in the Etcetera magazine.

Rochechouart:

In March 2013, Samantha organised a surprise for us. It is an overnight stay away in a local hotel. One of her necessary criteria in researching somewhere to send us, as a Mother's Day treat, is that it must have a bath. Nigel and I are not good at accepting charity. Samantha knows this, but she also knows about the tensions at home in our confined quarters. Nigel and I get little quality alone time, or privacy to talk, so this kind gesture is graciously accepted and is very welcome.

The hotel is in the centre of Rochechouart, a picturesque, walled town about thirty minutes' drive from Limoges. Rochechouart, situated in the Haute-Vienne, Dept. 87 is about thirty minutes' drive from our house in Chirac. Its old world charm oozes from every cobble in the beautiful streets. Rustic charm seeps out like the moss over damp walls, from every stone in the haphazardly constructed houses. Overshadowing the town centre is the castle that looks as though it has popped up out of a scene from a Disney film like Sleeping Beauty. It was allegedly once the home of the Viscount of Rochechouart and even has a drawbridge. Legend has it that its destruction was ordered during the French Revolution. However, the extreme ruggedness of the stonework held off the bombardment. We are yet to explore in detail the history of the town. I read that one of the largest meteorites ever to hit the earth, over two hundred million years ago, landed here.

When Samantha and Cam return from Australia, for two weeks at the end of October 2013, we arrange a couple of trips to tourist hotspots. We take the recommendations of friends and neighbours, to go to places that we have yet to visit. Thus, we enjoy the new experiences together as a family.

Oradour Sur Glane:

On the 29th October, we drive to Oradour Sur Glane with Samantha and Cam. This village fifteen minutes' drive from Limoges in Department 87, is the site of an unusual memorial museum. It provides a memorial to the people killed, and preserves the remains of a small village, that was the site of a war atrocity in 1944. The original population was wiped out on 10th June 1944. The people living there at that time numbered six hundred and forty two. The Germans massacred almost all, including the women and children. After the war, the president of France at the time, Charles De Gaulle, ordered that a new village be built on an adjacent area of land, and that the remnants of the old village be preserved.

The story goes that the Germans believed that the Resistance in Oradour Sur Vayres, a neighbouring village, was holding an officer, an alleged SS Commander. They believed the Resistance captured him the previous day.

On 10th June, the Germans surrounded Oradour Sur Glane, after confusing it with nearby Oradour Sur Vayres. After congregating the townspeople and any visitors to the town that day in the village square, they commenced checking their papers. They moved the women and children to the church, whilst they pillaged the village. Meanwhile, they led the men to six barns and sheds where machine guns were already in place. All, men women and children, were slaughtered.

As we enter to go through to the village remains, we walk through a museum. Here the rooms are filled with information on the village, in English and French. It tells of the Germans and the backstory to the massacre. We then reach a screen room or small theatre. As I did not consider what to expect here, which in hindsight is naive given the background to the museum, we sit and watch old black and white footage of the horrific aftermath. Some of the images, although not graphic, hid nothing of the intended message. I sit, resisting the urge and sensation to be sick as I try to avert my eyes, not wanting to disturb everyone else by walking out. Equally, I do not want to vomit on the floor. Thankful that it is a short film, as we exit the room I am glad the door to outside and fresh air is nearby. As we walk towards the village centre the remains of burnt out cars, prams and bicycle frames in the streets is haunting. The sewing machines and cooking appliances are still in place, yet abandoned by the destruction of fire in the houses.

The air is clear; it is almost seventy years since the fiery destruction, but the sights and eerie silence convinces my brain otherwise. It is stifling. There is a story of a survivor, who said that the German soldiers shot the men in the legs. The injuries were bad enough for them to die a slow painful death, and rendered them unable to move. They were then doused in fuel and set fire too. Six men were believed to have escaped, although one was later shot dead in the cemetery. In total, 190 men were killed. The women and children, who had been herded into the church, were set alight with explosives. As they tried to escape through the church windows, they were gunned down by machine guns. Two hundred and forty -seven women and two hundred and five children died in the slaughter. By nightfall, the village was almost destroyed.

As we walk the streets of this desecrated village, Nigel and Samantha take photographs, as the skies darken. Was this a sign? Were we disrespecting the memory of the people who suffered here by taking photographs? The rumbles of distant thunder add to the macabre atmosphere, and we decide we have seen enough and head back to the car. As we walk towards the exit gate, with the view of the new church built in the new village in front of us, the heavens open. Torrential rain causes water to cascade down the sloping roads towards the car park. Back in the car, soaked and feeling subdued we decide to head straight home.

Brantome:

On 31st October 2013, we organise a visit to Brantome for an overnight stay. We had visited this quaint riverside town before with Clair when she came over, but only for a day trip. We felt it warranted a longer stay this time. Our plan is to incorporate a visit to the popular Brantome Friday Market. As it is Halloween night, we get a special offer and book two rooms at the Hotel Charbonnel. The River Dronne winds its way through this exquisite town. Brantome is home to the Abbey, which when lit up at night, is chilling yet magnificent. The shadows it casts make you imagine that the ghosts of monks are watching you from the windows that tower above you.

At the hotel, each room had a small balcony terrace so we can sit and people watch across the river over glass of wine. As we check in, they give us the keys and say that one room is on the first floor, the other on the second floor. Since I was the one who made the room bookings, I thought the rooms to be identical. Therefore, graciously we let the others take the room on the first floor. We follow the porter, who is escorting us, up to the second floor. Excitedly looking around our room as we do on these special rare outings, I am immediately deflated as I see we have a shower and no bath. We arrange to drop our bags ready to head out for a walk around the town. It is late afternoon so maybe we will stop for a glass of wine somewhere, as we will be going out for dinner after eight this evening. As we are always ready first, we go to their room to hurry them up. As usual, because I am nosey, I start to look around only to find their room has a bath. No, they did not offer to swap. How rude! Only kidding Samantha and Cam.

Although the hotel has a well renowned restaurant, specialising in regional cuisine, we opt for a small restaurant we passed whilst out walking, making a reservation for eight o'clock. Nigel and I have not been out for dinner since March so I am excited about this. The meal and the service are exceptional and after a few more glasses of red wine in the hotel bar we retire for the night.

The following morning before attending the market we go for breakfast in a small coffee shop called La P'tite Bouffe. Samantha has crepes with chocolate sauce. When in France do as the French do, that was her excuse for having chocolate for breakfast. Nigel and I have a croque-monsieur. This resembles a toasted ham and cheese sandwich, except that they melt the cheese to the outside of the sandwich. There is a feminine version of this called the croque-madame which has a fried or poached egg on the outside of the toasted sandwich. Anyway, this delicious, melt in the mouth French delicacy, simple in structure, but big on taste compliments the freshly ground coffee. Revived from a hearty breakfast we are ready to explore the market. It consists of food stalls of every variety, clothing, books and gifts. I find a bargain two-euro bookstall and Nigel agrees to my ten-euro book budget leaving me to browse and buy as I please.

Brantome Abbey

Brantome has fascinated visitors over the years. It boasts caves, scenic boat trips, restaurants and above all tranquillity, despite being a tourist hotspot. The name Brantome apparently originates from a combination of Celtic words for water and rocks. The monastery evolved into an Abbey during the Renaissance period, when the Jardin Des Moines (Monk's garden) was added. This town is believed to be one of the world's most sacred sites and is a special place of enlightenment and healing for body and the mind. I certainly sensed this power as we walked through the town in the shadow of the Abbey and the caves.

Vide Greniers

When your budget for leisure pursuits is limited, finding things to do is tricky, but important when you are living and working on your house all week. Therefore, some creative thinking is needed. Looking for opportunities to practice our French language skills led us to visiting the local brocantes and vide greniers on Sundays over the summer months. The phrase vide grenier literally means 'empty attic' and brocantes are 'second hand goods in a shop or flea market.' Therefore, the similarity to English car boot sales has us hooked. This had always been a good weekend pastime for us when the children were small. We would give them all one pound in loose change to go and find the bargain of the day, to show at the dinner table later. It is funny how some things never change. When we decide to start attending the vide greniers and brocantes we are not searching for anything in particular, and we issue ourselves a strict budget, usually ten euros. The rules are that it must be useful or fit in with the rustic interior planned for the house when the renovations are complete.

Over the next few weeks, some of the purchases slip outside these rules in one way or another. Books that are not classified as useful by Nigel slide into my carrier bags. Jaime's purchases also sit outside the remit in some respects as she tries to develop her love of fashion designing. She starts buying skirts, blouses and dresses that she will individualise with her creative sewing talents. Unfortunately, most end up as rags, when they do not confirm to her exacting requirements or do not fit correctly. I cannot help noticing that many French people walk around carrying pieces of rusty metal and pots with obvious holes in them. Items that I perceive as junk must have some value to them. That said, by the end of the summer, I too have started seeing the beauty and functionality in similar items. I buy a metal fire bucket or cauldron, which will be a planter for my thyme, and old enamel dishes, which will collect water from my indoor plants. As they say, one man's trash is another man's treasure.

Marche de Nuit Montbron

Nicky and Tim invite us to meet them at the 'Montbron Night Market' in August. Montbron is about a fifty-minute drive from our house. In France, it does not seem to matter how rural a town or village is, over the summer there is usually something amazing going on. This event is widely talked about, so we decide to treat ourselves to an evening out. However, the snippets of conversation and articles I read about it made it sound like a small artisan trade show. Therefore, when we arrive and signs indicate for us to park on the outskirts of the town in a field, as the gendarmes have closed off all the streets, we know we have underestimated the size and popularity of the event. We arrange to meet Tim and Nicky outside the bank in the market square but to get there we walk through streets jam-packed with stalls with many more down each side street. There is no dedicated route to follow to ensure you see everything, so after meeting up we just walk around letting our senses be seduced by either the delicious smell of food on offer, or the sight of glittering or interesting items on the stalls. Nicky spots a handbag she likes, but she wants a bargain so she manages to barter with the French man for a reduction in price. I hope I can do that next year.

The variety of stalls is awesome, from jewellery to knitted gifts, clothing of all descriptions, books, paintings, witchcraft items and more soap and scented candle stalls than I have ever seen in one market, and we probably did not see the whole market. It is a warm evening, and I have my first introduction to a French tipple, which is a favourite with Tim and Nicky, called a demi-peche. It is French beer with a dash of peach syrup added. Whatever it is, it goes down a bit too easily. Sitting in the evening sun, we watch an ice sculptor at work making dolphins, and roses that start to melt quicker than he expected. Musicians and street entertainers perform on street corners. On the main stage, the variety of entertainers has something for everyone with all genres from jazz to choir singing accommodated. In addition to the bars, restaurant and cafes opening their doors for the night, there is a huge variety of street food stalls scattered throughout the town. Everything from barbeques to artisan food stalls selling cheese or crepes. The Montbron Night Market was a combination of multi-cultural people, strange stalls, interesting stalls, street entertainers, and an exceptional array of culinary delights. We had a fun night.

CHAPTER 15 FAMILY LIFE CHANGING LANES

Happy days, Nigel & Jaime in Hobart, Tasmania

Diary of a difficult relationship: Nigel and Jaime
As I try, unsuccessfully, to escape from the concrete maze, in this recurring dream I get very little rest. This dream haunts me, not just then but now. What is the hidden meaning? Subtle, yet hard-hitting change is instant and unforgiving. The challenging life experiences we face emulate rowing a boat against the tide trying to reach calmer waters. Weakness in a relationship exposes raw emotions. The mix is volatile, like a poorly researched chemistry experiment. In reality, it is not any worse than the behaviour we encountered with the older children as teenagers. Well, that is how I rationalise it to Nigel during the testing times, hoping his memory does not serve him as well as mine. However, in this claustrophobic setting the effects become amplified in intensity. With no extended family to ease the strain of one on one difficult relationship, it is a powder keg waiting to explode, or my shaken soda bottle scenario again like in Alice Springs.

Tolerance, patience and understanding are in short supply at the time they are needed the most. When you are in the midst of experiencing hard, personally challenging times, it is sometimes difficult to think about anything else. It becomes all-consuming in both your waking and dream time. Dealing with the challenges, minute by minute, hour by hour, soon becomes day by day and week by week. Before you realise it months pass and the strain of this endurance exercise is clear for everyone to see. Then, in what appears to be a sudden epiphany, you realise that some of the challenges you were facing have eased, resolved or just been overtaken by a new challenge. I stop and wonder how, when and why, usually to no avail, that is until I reach for my diaries. Here lie the answers and the lessons to learn from these challenging times. I often get these epiphany moments. I use them to pinpoint important changes in my mindset and personal coping mechanisms so that I learn from every experience.

It is these life lessons that are brought to the fore during this difficult period that Nigel, Jaime and I, by default, are enduring. So much hurt, resentment, guilt and anger exists between them. So much so, that it forms a wall preventing them from moving forward. Sometimes they cannot even bear to look at each other or be in the same room. This is difficult in our current environment where escape is futile especially during the winter months. In reality, we both know that Jaime never intended to hurt Nigel with her decision-making. Deep down, sometimes too deep, Nigel does love her, even though they will always need to work harder to achieve the close bond that he has with the other children. The cause of that problem in their relationship does not result from her decision making. It originates from her genetic makeup which neither she or Nigel can change.

As you can imagine, Jaime, in addition to recovering from her latest CRPS episode, is dealing with emotional and psychological trauma. Yes, some of it is self-inflicted by her decision making. However, the reality is that her biological father, whom she so wanted to bond with, has let her down; it is a sad fact to face. Any normal parent would expect that he would take this opportunity and go out of his way to prove I had been wrong about him for all these years. However, all he proved was that he has no genuine feelings of love for Jaime and no concern for her wellbeing. On her return to us, Jaime is on a low dose of antidepressants. This vital part of her pain management therapy also initially helps her cope mentally. She needs to come to terms with the consequences of where she now finds herself, in a cottage in rural France, with no proper bathroom, no mobile network coverage and no internet. Life without these basic requirements, for a teenage girl, becomes hellish for all involved. As the pain therapy comes to an end, the realisation dawns that life is going to be a lot harder. On the social, educational and physical level the harsh realities of her new life in France dawn on her and us. Jaime withdraws into herself once again. Obviously, Nigel is supportive of her return home; it was his idea. However the pre-existing problems in his relationship with Jaime remain. In our small, cramped environment with few amenities, our lifestyle now means that for a teenage girl and a hurting stepfather, emotions run at fever pitch. Explosive encounters erupt over the most trivial things.

With the help of my friend Julia, her husband Phil and son Andrew, we try to access schooling or some form of education for Jaime. Our goal being that she can learn French, meet and socialise with people of her own age. However, if I thought her dyslexia was an issue in the UK or Australia I had completely underestimated how much of a problem it would be here in France. It soon becomes clear that finding a school environment is not going to work. Therefore we enrol Jaime on a distance-learning course in animal care. This has an amazing effect. It is giving her a focus, a reason to get up in the morning, something to do and to think about other than her social predicament. It is also a potential ticket to a life outside France, which has become her goal. The belief that she can gain a qualification to enable her to move to the UK motivates her. Her long held dream of undertaking an apprenticeship working with horses or animals now looks more achievable and realistic. The veil of sadness starts to lift. Over the next few months, we all work hard to help her find English speaking friends. She socialises with them at sleepovers and meetings at the local café to play pool. Despite her finding a small circle of friends, I know in my heart she will not be able to build a life here in France. The reality is that the day will dawn again when she leaves for pastures new.

Empty nesters: Jaime's story
In June 2013 after months of searching for live in apprenticeships in the UK, we eventually find one in Suffolk at an equitation centre. Jaime would start as a volunteer horse groom for three months whilst they assess her skills. She will need to integrate into life away from home living in a hostel with the other trainees from around the world. The process of letting her go again is hard, and this episode is not without its difficulties, but for now she is on a path of self-discovery, her confidence increasing and she is happy. What will I miss about Jaime? Her trivial chatter each morning when I am trying to write, Facebook gossip and tips on what music I should listen to are her favourite subjects of conversation.

"What shall I do today?" This is her regular question, which she asks every morning while eating her breakfast. It is as if she expects that something interesting, exciting or amazing has been planned overnight without her knowledge. I am her only true friend in this solitary existence that is now her life. I have to find time for her need to socialise even if she has to make do with the fact that her best friend is her mum. I have a visit planned to go and see her in September 2013 for her birthday, and I will take her on holiday for a week with her big brother Rob. We will catch up with family and friends and enjoy quality time together, mother and daughter. The bond that we have is very special. I still feel her pain, however remote we may be from one another. I am extremely grateful for this blessing.

Sally, my youngest sister, has been kind enough to collect Jaime from Stansted airport and have her stay for the couple of days of interviews and orientation. As they visit the equitation centre Sally's instincts are that she would not allow her children to live there. However, none of us can afford that luxury of choice. Jaime is again on the verge of depression in France and this opportunity, although a hard life lesson and not ideal, is her only way out. Is she running away? Yes. Am I stopping her? No. What kind of mother that does that make me? I know that I have to let her go as the only way of attempting to protect her mental well-being from the effects of life in France. I cannot and will not make her ride that roller coaster of mental anguish again.

As Jaime moves into the hostel after a successful orientation, as a mother I am worried about her as I consider my sister's concerns. However, I am concerned for her mental well-being, if she has to return to France. Between us, we have to make this work. I think that knowing we have our holiday to look forward to in September helps the transition and her daily updates are positive, and Facebook paints a picture of new friends and Jaime enjoying her horse riding again, after a shaky start. Here in France, although for me it is empty and quiet, for us, with our renovation project and plans for the garden, it is full steam ahead, business as usual. We are back to being empty nesters and cooking meals for two. We can enjoy a glass of wine in the evening sun, not needing to talk, as we are comfortable just in each other's presence. It is something that is hard to achieve with a teenager in the house. Teenagers have a need for constant noise or chatter whether it from the radio, television, or by demanding your attention. The Butfield world appears to be getting back on track. It is summer. The days are long; Nigel has labouring work with Tim and the sun shines as our beacon of hope. We have turned the corner and the good times, which we came to France for, are ahead of us now. The other children all have visits planned and there is so much to be excited about now. Therefore, with no more excuses, I need to get 'Glass Half Full' finished.

CHAPTER 16 WHEN ALL YOU WANT IS SOMEONE TO SAY "YES"

The hard truth is that I lack the confidence to self-publish. I doubt or do not believe strongly enough in my ability as a writer, storyteller and a conveyer of inspiration and positivity. What a contradiction in terms. I want to inspire and motivate people to be positive about the challenges which life throws at them. However, the irony is that I cannot find that in myself to publish a book they need to read to provoke this reaction. This is despite massive support and encouragement from family, friends, and fellow authors and readers on the networking site Autonomy. 'Glass Half Full' has been available, for members to read and comment on, for several months now and has produced comments like:

"Real life tales always make for the best reading. With Glass Half Full, author Sarah-Jane Butfield joins the pantheon of celebrated nonfiction biographers. In particular, the account is engaging from the start and draws the reader in with a combination of graphic scene descriptions and vibrant characters. You can almost taste and feel the Australian outback. Its tangibility is most evident in the sections that cover tribal customs, and near to desolate landscapes. You can't write fiction better than this." Clive Radford author of Doghouse Blues

"This is a great book. The tone with which you write is perfect for a biographical piece. You manage to story tell and not focus on you as much as give umbrella messages to the reader. Even though it is upsetting in places, it is equally heart-warming. You write in such a way that a reader does not need to have had your exact experiences to identify with the broader messages. Your writing is very polished. I especially liked your first Christmas in Australia. Having moved to Australia myself for some time it was Christmas for me too, which was a real pull on the heartstrings. It was the first huge recognition/realisation of being away from family and friends. BUT you manage to draw out the silver lining and see the glass as half full. This is a great book for anyone to read in tough times. Your descriptions are vivid and often beautiful." Laura author of Beneath the Blossom Tree and Vengeful Love

"A very rich story, well written. No matter what problems arise, you take them head on with determination. There was so much genuine emotion throughout. I like the way you set the scene and describe things, i.e. culture, places, buildings, lifestyle. Even down to the origin of Pommies! I empathize with you nursing in a hospital far removed from England. It was interesting reading about the aborigines and their wayward ways. I love camping, but certainly not, where snakes and dingoes visit. The bond between you and your daughter comes over well. I just like the way you knuckle down to life and despite the sadness enjoy what Alice Springs has to offer between working hard. A heartfelt enlightening story showing such determination in overcoming obstacles at all costs. Once again, your descriptions are florid which sets this story aside as you do not dwell on the bad. I loved reading about the locals and their lifestyle, the surroundings and beliefs. This is a well-written piece of work. It's difficult to do it justice in a review, but I could see, hear and appreciate all the emotion and want it all to work out for you as there is so much love between all the family members." Robyn Quaker author of Halfpennies and Blue Vinyl

"I want your life! What a wonderful rich voyage and you tell it so effortlessly. I have been reading it to my daughter; we are both really enjoying your story. Your writing style is so accessible and easy to read. I think you tick all the boxes, you give just the right amount of details never too much or too little, I think it is instinctual you are just a good storyteller. I love learning about Australia, the animals, the landscape, the weather it is all really interesting. Your family sound so wonderful, despite a tough start and difficult decisions." Lucy

Fellow authonomites have taken their manuscripts and produced self-published books. Their books are selling, and being reviewed, but here I am watching in awe. Waiting for what? Well, the dream, I suppose. My reluctance to, or fear of, self-publishing causes me to believe that the only way my story will be told is if I am accepted by traditional publisher. This will show that someone believes in my story and me. I would love my book to be available for others to read. That I know is a big ask for a debut author. Unless you are a celebrity or famous for something, the chances of a publisher or agent being interested in a biographical memoir is remote. 'Glass Half Full', in my opinion, is a niche market book. It may appeal to those who have or are considering migration to Australia. It may also appeal to people interested in the aftermath of natural disasters or people interested in the lives of other normal people in extraordinary circumstances and situations. Other readers may seek inspiration and motivation from reading a true story about a positive woman and her family overcoming adversity instead of succumbing to it.

Therefore, in my quest to find a publisher I research and consider carefully, appropriate publishers with experience in this niche area. It is also important that they provide a support package suitable for a debut author. This research is no mean feat on its own. Numerous vanity publishers disguise themselves as publishers, then only revealing their true colours after telling you they would love to read the manuscript. The alarm bells ring when they tell you how excited they are to promote your work without reading it and then comes; "Oh, by the way, this is the cost of publishing, marketing and promotion." The costs varied from hundreds to thousands. After months of looking and continuing to have 'Glass Half Full' proofread and amended, I shortlist two publishers. These are not vanity publishers, and they both have a reputation for taking good care of biographical and memoir writers. In preparation for making my submissions I read many books on how to be published. I read about how to edit and format for successful submissions to agents and publishers, and how to write successful query letters. As my knowledge grows, I attempt to apply all the rules laid out for success. The only exception being that I am not comfortable with multiple submissions. Therefore, I decide that even though it will take longer I will submit to one at a time.

Published authors proofread the required first three chapters, after I utilise free online sites like Grammarly and Paperrater to help with the editing of grammar and punctuation. It is a necessary part of sharing my writing experiences to show how my writing has been influenced by life events. Therefore, I will relate the story of receiving the news of my one and only memoir rejection. This in turn led to the process I used to move forward. For any aspiring authors reading this book, who maybe in a position of considering their publishing options, this is what they are interested in, how do you cope and deal with rejection? The day I receive the news I am not in France at home with my supportive husband. I am alone in a Premier Inn hotel room near Stansted Airport. I travelled from Limoges to Stansted on Sunday 9th September. The first leg of my visit to spend time with Rob; and to surprise Jaime for her upcoming seventeenth birthday celebrations. This next part is not entirely relevant to the story, but it gives an insight into my mind-set at the time. On arrival in Stansted Airport, I board a shuttle bus that goes to the nearby hotels.

"Is the bus going to the Premier Inn?" I ask the driver as I board.

"Yes: That's three quid; I'll let you know when we get there."

There are only two other people on the bus, who look like workers, not hotel visitors. They both get off at the Holiday Inn. Less than a minute later the bus pulls into a coach parking bay and stops. The driver turns off the engine and gets out of his cab. I get up and walk towards the doors, which are now open.

"Oh I forgot about you," he says turning as he hears my footsteps approaching him.

"That's ok I can walk from here." I say, in a typically stoic British fashion, not wanting to make a fuss.

However, inside my annoyance is growing at the failure of the driver to deliver on his word. I had been on the bus for less than six minutes. Am I, or is my need to know when I am at my hotel stop, that forgettable and unimportant to him? Are these selfish thoughts on my part? I am not that important and certainly not to a bus driver eager for his lunch break. Selfish is probably not the right word, I admit, as I write this in retrospect. However, at the time, in such a dreary setting, that is how exactly how I perceive it. I get off the bus and walk across the car park, becoming soaked through from the pouring rain and having no coat. The Premier Inn is now a welcoming oasis ahead of me. With an increased sense of being invisible to the outside world, and alone, I am too early to check into my room. I decide to get a Costa coffee from the café in the hotel foyer. I order a large cappuccino and find an armchair tucked away in a corner away from the television, which has Sky Sports on. I can hide with my Kindle and my coffee, the ultimate escapism.

Later in my hotel room, after a long soak in the bath, a luxury that I will repeat during my brief eighteen-hour overnight stay, I receive a very welcome text from Nigel saying 'Can you call me?' I make myself a cup of tea, and settle down for a chat. I am so excited to talk to him that I do not even consider that there is any specific reason that he has asked me to call. Nigel tells me that he has checked my emails as instructed and that there is an email from the publisher.

"Shall I open it?" He says. Excitement, rushes through me; why do I always think the best, most positive outcome? How arrogant I must be, or appear to be. Is that how others see my perceived positivity?

"Yes of course," I say as I lean back ready to listen. Nigel reads the content of the email that contains feedback on my submission, and constructive ideas for improvement. It ends with an offer to resubmit after a professional edit. This feedback is prompt, informative, and constructive, and I will need to take it on board if I am going to move forward. However, that does not suppress the emotions now welling up inside of me.

After some supportive, straight taking advice from Nigel, who, as always, keeps me on track, we say goodnight. I am left alone with my thoughts and the television again. As I sit there, I find myself rummaging in my handbag for my trusty notebook and pen, which are never far away. Whilst sitting on the bed, I spot the Gideon Bible on the bedside cabinet. I reach for it, turning to the front pages. It contains ready-made recommended readings for a multitude of life events when you may need some spiritual help. I am sure of this because I have a small version of this bible at home, which I refer to with increasing frequency of late. It is normally in my handbag; however, ironically it is not there on this needy occasion. There is no section in it for the author having their submission rejected, but there is a section for needing guidance.

Matthew Verse 7: "Ask, and it will be given to you. Seek, and you will find. Knock and the door will be opened for you. For everyone who asks receives, he who seeks finds and to he who knocks the door will be opened."

From that moment on it felt as if everything I heard or saw on television, or read, was willing me to fight for what I wanted to achieve. Even random song lyrics in adverts poked at my subconscious thoughts. As I continued scribbling in my notepad, my action plan began to form in front of me. Actions to take, and things to check about the submission I had made. Then a horrible truth dawns on me. I had been in a rush, for no good reason, to submit before coming away to the UK for a week. Now in the solitude of my hotel room and without my laptop here to check, I doubt which version of the manuscripts first three chapters I used in the submission. Had I made a schoolboy error and sent one of the many 'work in progress edits' without thoroughly checking? In a week's time, to my horror and embarrassment, the answer would be yes, but even so my book still needs some of the other changes identified in the rejection feedback. The proactive nature of writing a plan of action helps to refocus me. In addition, the act of spending the evening writing new material for this book is motivational, so these acts combined mean I am back on track. I am sure that I will achieve my dream of being a published author. However, I also recognise that maybe I will have to think outside the box and that I may need some professional help.

After my week in the UK away from my laptop, but not necessarily away from writing, I feel refreshed and motivated to achieve my publishing goals. I have made a decision. I no longer want to wait for someone to say 'Yes.' to my book and me. I am going to say 'Yes,' to myself. Believe in my own abilities and find the courage to self-publish my book.

"You're not really a threat to JK Rowling, but I know a lot of people will enjoy it." John, my father in law, has said this on more than one occasion after reading chapters of 'Glass Half Full'. At the end of the day, at least I am grounded, not expecting to become a best-selling author. My goal is simple, to be the author of a book that will provide inspiration to some and hope to others. Therefore, it begins. The journey from a manuscript on my laptop to published e-book and paperback on Amazon in six weeks.

CHAPTER 17 FAMILY TIME, FELIXSTOWE AND AN ANGRY RABBIT

More times than not when I have visited the UK since emigrating in 2008, it has rained or snowed. When I travelled from Australia, I expected opposite seasonal weather. Due to the cost, we often travelled during Australian summer, which is winter in UK. However, this time it is September and, until I left France, we had been enjoying long hot sunny days and balmy evenings in the garden. From the moment I land in Stansted it rains. As usual, I am ill equipped as I am travelling on a budget airline with just one rucksack as my hand luggage. As the weather was so good on the way to the airport, I arrived wearing only a thin fashion jacket. I confess to looking forward to my solo one night at the Stansted Premier Inn.

I indulge myself in Costa coffee whilst people watching. I become mesmerised by a woman who walks in alone. The short A line dress she is wearing is not complimenting her swollen, pregnancy filled legs, which resemble uncooked cocktail sausages. Her pale skin gathers below her knees as if it is restricting the fluid both above and below. The nurse in me wonders if her pregnancy is complicated by a medical condition causing her to have so much oedema, fluid in her legs. I watch to see if any of the men in the hotel coffee shop, with their business suits and laptops, will offer her a chair to rest those painful looking legs. Not one of them moves. I decide I will be the only person with some manners in the room, and I start to gather my belongings, gesturing to her as I do so. She smiles and points as she orders a takeaway coffee and leaves. I return to my Kindle reading.

During the afternoon and evening, I indulge myself with two, long overdue, soaks in bubbly hot baths. It has been six months since my last bath. I should state here that, as disgusting as that may sound, we do have a strip wash every day with our trusty pink Gifi bucket in our makeshift bathroom at home. My three-euro bargain bucket is lasting well. Despite at least twice daily use, so far it has escaped destruction usually caused by my clumsiness. I am notorious for falling on things, knocking things over and generally breaking things.

Refreshed by a good night's sleep, the following morning I am excited and check out early. I walk across the car park to the McDonald's restaurant next to the hotel where I am meeting Rob at eleven o'clock. Since we arrived in France, Rob has been to visit us, but this is my first trip to visit him. Since we re-joined the digital world with internet access by Tooway satellite, Rob and I chat on Google plus daily. We Skype every week, if his hectic London social life allows! It is wonderful to be so close to him again and to have the opportunity to take part in his life again. I have missed that. I think as a parent, it comes naturally to me to care for my children, to be the one who does things for them, organising and taking care of everything. Therefore, when Rob announces he is arranging to hire a car, meet me at Stansted and drive us to Swilland to surprise Jaime, it takes me out of my usual parental control comfort zone. When I tell my friends about his plans they all say, 'Hey enjoy it,' so I intend to. When Rob walks into McDonald's and puts his arms around me, a surge of motherly love flows through every inch of my body. Even though boys are not well known for their public displays of affection, especially with their parents, Rob holds me in his strong protective embrace. I am overcome with pride. Rob has matured into an intelligent young man. He works for a global IT company in London, a job he hankered after for over a year. He worked towards getting the qualifications he needed whilst doing bar work to pay the bills. Now my son is here, taking charge, caring for his mum and younger sister for a week. He has made all the arrangements, and this is a surreal, yet comforting experience.

I do not like travelling alone. I knew I would have many demons to face on this trip due to my driving anxiety, Firstly because I make a horrendous passenger, especially being in an unfamiliar car. Secondly, Rob has only been driving for a couple of years, and this would be my first experience as his passenger. I did not doubt his skill or ability, but I did doubt my ability to put him at his ease, with me beside him. I have two bad habits; one is sinking my fingernails into the leather seats and upholstery, the second is pretending to brake, with no dual controls. Both of which are often commented on. Nigel is the only person who can drive with me as a passenger without inducing high level of anxiety, but the driving anxiety is never totally absent.

"What can I get you?" Rob says, as we release from our mother and son embrace.

I know I am smiling as I reply "I'll have a long black, oh and two sweeteners, please."

As I watch him walk confidently towards the counter, he stops to pick up the fallen Happy Meal toy of a small child secured in a high chair to his right. I am overcome with raw maternal emotions of love, pride and a degree of parental satisfaction that we have produced such an amazing young man. Rob returns with the coffees, and we chat about my journey from France, his journey from the car-hire pick-up point and our schedule for the day's events. We have devised a cunning plan to surprise Jaime, who thinks I am arriving later today and hence I am unable to see her until Tuesday. We will drive up to the stables in Suffolk where she is working as a volunteer until her apprenticeship begins in two weeks' time. After conspiring with her colleagues, we know she will be in the canteen on site on her lunch break at one o'clock. The journey should take us about an hour; we have plenty of time, but I am eager to get going. Neither Rob nor I have been to this remote part of Suffolk before, but Rob is confident that the Google maps app on his smartphone will get us there. However, he did not factor in my novice skills with smart phones or my inability to read maps. The phrase 'pinch and spread the screen mum,' is now indelibly imprinted on my brain. After driving through torrential rain and having to pull over three times for Rob to consult Google map, or reset the smart phone map after my accidently turning it off and opening a game app, we eventually arrive at a muddy yet sunny riding stables.

I am, of course, suitably ill equipped for this visit in my white espadrille sandals which darken in colour as we make our way through the stable yards to the canteen. Jaime's friends have manipulated the seating arrangements to ensure her back to the door. We enter and, sneaking up behind her, I put my arms around her neck. She jumps up, and the tears begin.

"I knew it was you, by the mummy perfume," Jaime says.

"Thanks, I think." Considering the canteen's ambience of horses, manure and greasy food, I wonder how she could have smelt anything.

Her face is dirty, and the tears form snaking rails through the dirt and makeup. Her hair smells of horse manure, and her uniform, a green sweatshirt, and beige jodhpurs look like she has worn them for days. Which she may well have done, without her mother's influence around to instruct her to wash them. Despite this, we hug each other. She is sobbing.

"You're cruel mummy, why didn't you tell me?"

"Well, it wouldn't be a surprise, if I'd told you, now would it?"

Then she spots Rob, who walks in behind me, and I am unceremoniously released, like an unwanted dress size on the changing room floor in a dress shop. She jumps into his arms and is spun around as he holds onto her waist. Rob used to do this to her when she was six. Back then, he would spin her around, and then let her go, ready to laugh, as she fell over disorientated. As he deposits her down his face gives his thoughts away, 'I smell like a horse now, thanks Sis.' Jaime takes us on an unwelcome tour of her bed space in the hostel, which is pretty grim. The selective photographs I had received did not reveal the level of detritus that occupies every corner of this makeshift home they call a hostel. The kitchen is strewn with dead flies, on the worktop and floor. The shower room is an orangey brown colour from years of scale and mould. The door hangs lifeless from the washing machine, as if it were a relic in the scrap yard, although Jaime reassures me that it still works. The stained and sodden carpet in front of it tells a less efficient story of its abilities.

As Jaime has to return to work, even though she is a volunteer they deemed it impossible for her to take the afternoon off, we say our tearful goodbyes. We make our plans to collect her tomorrow and set off to find our accommodation for the week, a self-catering caravan in Felixstowe.

Felixstowe holds many wonderful memories from my childhood, and it is thirty minutes' drive from Swilland. We arrive too early to collect our keys, so we drive to the seafront for some salty chips and a nostalgic look out to sea. Rob, who has developed an interest in photography, is on the lookout for photo opportunities while I sit and reminisce over the many Sundays in my childhood when our mum would bring us here on day trips. We would swim in the sea, play on the beach or under the pier, and visit the Sunday market before falling asleep in the car on the way home; happy days. When four o'clock comes, we return to the Park Holidays Felixstowe Beach Caravan Park and get the keys and a map. The receptionist assures us that we can drive to the caravan, but as we approach, it is clear that with the amount of rain recently here, to attempt this could be costly in a hire car. Parking on a nearby concrete base that a caravan had been from, we walk with our minimal luggage and let ourselves in. To say it is basic is an understatement, but it is cheap, and it is only a base. We decide to pop into town to the local Tesco's supermarket for some basic provisions. Tea, coffee and food for an evening meal, as we are sure that the menu at the bar and restaurant on site will consist of fried food. As we had chips on the seafront earlier, we want something a bit more nutritious for dinner. It has been a long time since I shopped with Rob for food. Therefore, our Tesco's trip today makes me realise that he is now an independent, capable young man. That said, he is a single man and as such heads straight for the beers and ready meals. I could not help but smile to myself, as he doubled back when he saw me at the greengrocery section.

Over the next couple of days, we have a huge dose of family life in a variety of forms. On the first night, we meet up with Molly and her boyfriend. It is amazing. Even though it was prearranged, I did not dare to believe, until she arrives, that it would actually happen. The basic ability to hold my little girl tightly in my arms, a mother holding her daughter, restores our connection, albeit short lived. We spend the early evening chatting with her about work, friends and where they live. Although the conversation is strained at first, as we skirt around topics that may involve her father, my heart warms as I glimpse the twinkle in her eyes as she talks about topics that excite her like her beauty business; that is my little girl. Her mannerisms are identical to Jaime, even though they were not brought up together. She has a sparkle, is hard working, and she loves life. As we continue chatting the children's entertainers come into the bar. One of them is wearing a large rabbit costume. The rabbit, escorted by a young woman, jogs from table to table as she develops a worried look on her face. Instead of being happy and jolly, this rabbit has some issues. He is knocking things off the tables, clearing whole tables by sliding his costume-enclosed arm across them. At times, he appears out of control, throwing leaflets and salt and pepper sachets into the air. As he approaches, our table we are smiling yet apprehensive as the angry man in a rabbit costume stands behind Molly. She sits very still. Luckily, we escape with just our table contents being thrown to the floor. The rabbit spoke with an Eastern European accent, possibly Polish but whatever his nationality I think he is not happy in his work.

Jaime taking selfies in the caravan with mum photobombing!

The next day we collect Jaime, who is ready for a few days of birthday celebration activities. These include birthday shopping for gifts and clothes, some nice meals, and the family get together in the clubhouse at the caravan park on her birthday. We visit my sister Susie and her family for a roast dinner one evening, and catch up with the whole family. They have not seen Rob for a while, and it is great to see all the nieces and nephews together. Darren, Susie's husband, is glad of a new man with whom to discuss his new pastime of metal detecting. They plan a trip to the beach for the following evening.

My sister Susie, seated and unaware of the face Jaime is pulling!

On Jaime's birthday, we meet Susie and her family, and Molly and her boyfriend in the clubhouse at the caravan park. It is a surreal experience, being in the same room as Rob, Jaime and Molly. However, it is tinged with sadness that Nigel and Samantha are not there to complete my little family unit. Early in the evening, after the daily bingo session ended, the children's entertainment starts in the main hall. Guess who is the main attraction? I mean apart from Jaime as she sports a huge badge saying 'I'm 17 today' which has most of the young men in the bar looking at her. Yes, you guessed it, the angry rabbit on the rampage again. He takes a liking to Susie, probably because of her gorgeous abundance of auburn hair, which has always been an attraction since she was a child. The rabbit loiters near to our table waving and putting his head behind members of our party whilst Darren and Rob try to take photographs. Luckily, tonight his behaviour is limited to being a bit flirty with the parents of the kids who have come to watch him perform.

Our few days together disappear quickly and effortlessly like an autumnal gust of wind. After returning Jaime to her friend's house, Rob takes me to Stansted to catch my flight back to France. For the first time, I did not want to go back to France. Despite missing Nigel, the boys, my house and garden, the pain of leaving the children in the UK tears into my heart. I envy Susie with her children living so close to her. I question my rationale for continuing our latest quest. .Once on board the aircraft, I turn to my trusty notebook to record my feelings and to brainstorm why I feel like this. Am I being reactive? Probably. I should go home and settle back into my life. The children all have their own lives, they come and see us whenever they want or need to, so maybe it is just my maternal heartstrings being over stretched. Despite this surge of emotions, it is comforting to walk across the tarmac at Limoges and see Nigel waiting at the fence. As always, he is waving furiously as if I have been away for months instead of a week. Home sweet home.

CHAPTER 18 MOTHERS AND DAUGHTERS

I miss the children. Even though we now live closer to them, it does not feel any easier. I know they are not children anymore, but I will always be their mum or step-mum. Whatever their age or wherever they are, thoughts of them linger in my mind. I can start talking about them at random whilst we are working on the house or out and about. Things like, 'Rob would love to get a photo of that,' if we are visiting somewhere with interesting architecture. Or 'Clair would love it here,' if we find a new place to stop for coffee, where we can sit outside, and people watch. 'We must bring Sam and Cam here when they come over,' if I get a leaflet or information on somewhere new to visit. The list is endless.

The children, especially the girls, use me as the proverbial shoulder to cry on, or lean on in tough or challenging times. The bonds created in our family are the most powerful of all relationships. Motherhood and the associated emotional journey is one of the few things that can reduce me to tears, usually at the drop of a hat, or in reality on receipt of a text message. It must be my age; as the children get older, and become more responsible for their own unprompted actions, sending an unexpected text to say, 'I love you mum,' makes me smile. Wherever I am, or whatever I am doing, sometimes tears of pride flow freely. A new family saying is developing, 'Mum's eyes are leaking, again!' Maybe it is a woman thing, but I do worry more about the girls. I think mothers are always harder on their daughters. I think it is because as a woman, and a mother, I have been where they are in their lives, and know the potential dangers. A mother's instinct is to protect her children whatever sex they are. However, as they get older, I feel less able to protect them from harm as they start making their own decisions. This makes me worry more because I know they will, and need to, make their own mistakes.

As a mum, step mum and a grandmother-to-be this year, I scrutinize myself more than is healthy. The thought of becoming my mother is a scary prospect. I look in the mirror sometimes and see small, yet unmistakable similarities to her mannerisms and looks, but that is not what scares me. I am proud to have some of her looks. She always took great care of her appearance. I remember the skin on her face, soft like velvet as I kissed her goodnight, her make-up, always perfect whatever the occasion. A hard working woman, her hands told the tale, with dry and cracked skin that caught on my wool cardigan as she got me ready for school. However, part of me does not want to be like her. As a teenager and a young woman, I was sure of the qualities I would replicate from my upbringing. I also knew those which I would relegate to the realms of mistakes of a past generation. My biggest wish would be to have known her much better as a woman. However, her health and circumstance meant that she passed away before we enjoyed those times. These rambling thoughts tumble around in my head as I ponder the various relationships with my girls. I think mothers are always harder on their daughters because they know what they are capable of.

Jaime, the youngest and the last to leave home, had been essentially an only child since 2008, when we moved to Australia. Jaime and I enjoy a lot of quality time together, just the two of us. In happy times, we have travelled, shopped and been ladies that lunch in Sydney, Melbourne and Hobart. We laugh a lot. In times of ill health, I nurse her back to health after abscess surgery in Alice Springs in 2010. I teach and help her with daily wound care for five months. Then I support and encourage her as she comes to terms with the permanent scarring left as a reminder. I have slept in hospital beds with her during many admissions for episodes of her CRPS. While enduring these challenging personal experiences together, we forged a bond, which needs no words or explanation. I know that at times this bond can cause friction with some of the other children. They do not always fully understand her, or her condition, and at times it looks like attention seeking behaviour. I understand their frustration, but experiencing it with her, I empathise with Jaime's anger when they doubt her. Sometimes all a girl wants from her mum is a hug, a hot water bottle and a cup of tea. The sympathy or empathy for their current dilemma or challenge is always unconditional. However, when it comes to teenage dramas, she is no different to the others. If I am missing clothes, makeup or jewellery I need look no further than Jaime's room to find them.

To survive with their sanity intact, mothers have to believe that the girl's teen phase will pass quicker than the years. Jaime has worked hard to try to fit back into UK life, but her heart lies in Australia. If we are honest, she was never happy about leaving Hobart in the first place. This was demonstrated by her knee-jerk reaction when we announced our French plans. Jaime has made plans to return to Australia in 2014, the year of her eighteenth birthday, to live and work amongst her friends in Queensland and Tasmania. It will be a huge wrench for me; my baby girl now literally on the other side of the world again. How will she cope when she next struggles with her CRPS? How will I cope with her absence? My family unit that I keep trying to pull back together does not seem to want to knit together, instead it has its own shape to form, and I have to wear it.

Samantha, now a grown woman at the age of twenty-six, has experienced hurt in the form of divorce. For the last two years, she has been pursuing her own dreams, and adventures, by travelling around Australia with Cam. They have been working their way through their own extreme bucket list antics. These include activities like skydives, remote island jet skiing and tropical rainforest camping in North Queensland, to name but a few. Samantha and Cam announced their engagement after a romantic trip to Magnetic Island on 9th August 2013. They hope to settle in Australia one day. They have returned to the UK where the plan is for Cam to obtain a qualification on the skills needed list. That way, when and if they decide to return later on, they can have an easier and cheaper form of entry. I am so proud of Samantha and her determined attitude to do, see and achieve as much as possible. Our special bond, formed in my years as a single mum, when she and Rob were young, remains as strong as ever. She is looking forward to becoming a mother herself in November 2014, and I cannot wait to be a grandmother. Good times lay ahead for us all. Samantha and Cam are currently living and working in South Wales.

Clair my step daughter lives in Colchester, Essex. She is a funny and intelligent young woman and is a credit to Nigel and her mum. She is currently in the second year of her children's nursing degree at Anglia Ruskin University. Clair has been to France twice to stay and visit, and she loves the peace and tranquillity here. She always says, "I feel so chilled out here." That is probably because there is nothing else for visitors to do than relax, eat nice food, drink fine wine and enjoy the weather. Clair is very close to Nigel. Seeing them together laughing, pulling faces or even having a serious conversation is heart-warming. She loves flying to France; it is her 'little adventure' as she calls it. On her own with her trolley case, she drinks coffee in the departure lounge, and does people watching like her dad on the airplane. She looks like a proper 'lady about town' as she confidently crosses the runway in Limoges or Poitiers on arrival. It is an extremely proud feeling. As a step-mother, or parent in a blended family, as we are referred to these days, it is important to remember that flesh and blood alone does not make a relationship, but the love in a mother's heart does.

Sarah Jane & Molly

As is the way in life, where there are amazing highs, there will be devastating lows. My estranged daughter Molly contacted me in September 2013, just before I travelled to the UK for Jaime's birthday celebrations. It was as if all my prayers were answered in one Facebook message. I always hoped, believed and imagined the day we might finally be able to be mother and daughter, as I am with the other girls. We started communicating via Facebook. Molly agreed to meet in Felixstowe, to attend Jaime's birthday celebrations with my sister's family. At that moment, I was overcome with relief that no lasting damage had caused by our enforced separation. However, a few months later and we are estranged again. A mother and daughter may go through periods when they are not close or not even talking to each other, but deep down they can never stop loving each other. In the words of Pamela Dugdale, "Mothers learn early on that daughters will do what they want; all a mother can do is stand by to pick up the pieces." What will the girls take forward from my parenting skills as the years pass, and they continue their journey into womanhood and possibly parenting? There is no rule book, no instruction guide to being a mum. We are supposed to follow our maternal instincts, caring and nurturing new life to form healthy, loving and happy children. I know not all the girls have lived full time with me, but my role as a mum and step mum has remained the same throughout. I strive to make them happy. Sometimes I am successful, sometimes I make mistakes but being a mum is for life, and there are many years and occasions still to come for me to continue nurturing and just being there for them whenever they need me. It really is the hardest, yet most fulfilling and rewarding job on earth being a mum. .I once read a quote from an unknown author in a book about family relationships; it likened the relation of a mother and her daughter to the lottery. "In the lottery of life, my daughters are the six winning numbers and the bonus ball."

CHAPTER 19 AN INDIE AUTHOR'S DREAM A REALITY

Among my personal highlights of our first year in France has to be writing and publishing my debut book 'Glass Half Full: Our Australian Adventure'. On 15th November 2013, I click the publish button on Kindle Direct Publishing. I did not prepare for this moment. I was so wrapped up in the writing process, and reading about how to make the manuscript acceptable for publication, that I had skipped all the sections on marketing. That had to come later; there must be a book to sell first, surely. After submitting, the book then came the waiting, which I had planned for by way of a few glasses of red wine and going to bed. During my restless sleep, I repeatedly go over the process and the day's events in my mind. The publishing confirmation from Amazon arrived in my inbox just under twelve hours later. What have I done?

It is a scary business to put the innermost secrets of your life in a book for the world to look at and cast an opinion on. The flip side is the surge of pride that comes seeing my book cover and my name on my Kindle screen where I normally see other authors. For the last few weeks, as I worked on completing the editing and formatting, after getting copious notes from my beta readers, I have thought or spoken about little else. Getting the manuscript ready for the various platforms on which my book is now for sale is no mean feat. I even got to the stage of talking to myself, while sitting alone at a table in the area of the cave that is now our dining room. I would say to myself repeatedly, like a willing mantra, 'I can do this,' or 'Sarah just sit down and do it.' When procrastination came creeping in, I had to stay strong. When things get tough, or the IT elements of the process push me to the point of closing the laptop, I can make boring household tasks appear important enough to pull me away from these crucial final stages of book production. It is quite a surreal experience when a week later I am holding a physical copy of the book I have written. The day it arrives Nigel tricks me. I received the tracking email that said delivery would be Friday, but on the Thursday Nigel went to the door when the post woman knocked.

"Is it my book?"

"No." he says with no expression so I return to my late attempt at book marketing, as he walks across the room. "Only kidding!" he shouts as he rushes towards me. My heart is pounding as I struggle to open the brown cardboard packaging. Then I cry as I see my book, with my name on it in my hands. Nigel hugs me.

"How does that feel?" He is eagerly looking at me, but I am too choked up to speak. "Proud of you," he says, which makes me cry more.

First edition paperback cover

Then to have people asking me to sign their copies of my book, a few weeks later, is the stuff of dreams, my dreams. Every time someone emails me about our story with comments, thoughts or just good wishes, I feel blessed. This opportunity to fulfil a long held dream of writing and publishing a book is my little miracle. It has not been an entirely smooth journey and in that respect the direction of the book mirrors our life. It changes direction many times, especially in the early stages of the first and second draft. My beta reader team headed up by Nigel are harsh critics. Everything from the chronological order to my so-called black and white imagery, are in question as they dissect it to the nth degree. A writer's life in France is a solitary occupation. Even more so, when you consider that I complete my work in a house under renovation, which is a building site. I admit that there are occasions when I get angry and frustrated. Especially when I compromise on my writing time, and my self-imposed tight schedule. Interruptions become the norm. Sometimes it seems like my writing work is invisible and impossible. Then I realise that I am procrastinating, which is not allowed, and I should 'JDI' 'just do it' as we say in our family.

My writing, in whatever form it takes, keeps me focused on the bigger picture, 'living my dreams.' The biggest being that of becoming a published author. In 2012, that dream, represented by a Post-it note on my conceived dream board, is now a Post-it note on my achieved dreams board. However, I do not want to be merely a published author. I want to help and inspire others to not only write, but also to live their dreams. My work takes the form of memoir writing, blogging about my writing experiences and compiling self-help guides. To keep my writing aspirations firmly in place on the dream boards, it helps having so many projects still to complete.

My dream boards are a mess to an outsider. They consist of photographs, quotations and magazine cuttings, pretty much anything that inspires or motivates me. It is about not only me and my personal goals. I stick samples of home furnishings for our house, and ideas for how I want to spend my retirement. Books I want to read, movies I want to watch and people I would like to meet. It is the contents of my headspace struggling for some semblance of order on a large piece of a cardboard box. When I achieve one of my dreams, it is celebrated on the achieved dreams board, thus providing ongoing motivation and proof that dreams do come true. Therefore, I work my way, in no particular order, through the dreams. Of course, I believe in them all, or they would not be on there. Some, I know, will be more challenging than others, but as long as they are on the board all things are possible.

Before I published 'Glass Half Full' on Amazon, I had no real concept of how many types of e-readers there were on the market, which ones were the most popular or which distribution channels linked to them. It continues to be a huge learning curve for me, but every day I learn something new. Since the day of publication, I still find it hard to sleep. I am thinking about the book constantly. I read that writing a book is the easy part and then the hard work begins. Never a truer statement read in the writing arena. Once published, your next task is to market it and get it in front of your readers. As a debut author, totally focused on the end product I shielded myself from this part of the process. In hindsight, this is somewhat naive. To assume that sales will just happen is like believing in magic. Despite all this, I publish with no grand marketing plan in place. There are no pre-release promotions scheduled or websites featuring news of my book. Therefore, I am playing catch up from day one in the marketing stakes. I decide to watch, learn and follow other successful indie authors. In the pursuit of my dream, I am the proverbial sponge, soaking up information from any resource. Despite my lack of planning, ninety books are sold in the first two weeks on Amazon UK alone. I am very pleased with that. Who knows what I would be selling if I had planned for the release. Note to self; get organized for the sequel release.

After publishing with Amazon for Kindle and Createspace for the paperback, the other major platform to conquer is Smashwords. The aptly named process called the 'meat grinder' resembles the game Candy Crush saga. To be published, the manuscript file is scrutinised at many levels. If it successfully completes each level, it can move onto the next stage. Successful completion of this game means your book can be distributed to companies like Apple, Barnes & Noble, Kobo and Sony. As my learning curve continues to climb, I am continuing to work at making 'Glass Half Full' available on as many platforms as possible. Therefore, I also published through Bookbaby to give exposure on eSentral, Copia, Gardners and Oyster. It takes approximately four weeks to go live after file delivery is confirmed to these companies. I had no real concept of readers, other than friends and family, being interested in reading about our experiences. However, it has been an amazing experience to have other people read our story, email me and offer advice and support. It is quite a surreal experience. It is still amazing to think that total strangers become fans when you write about your life and experiences. My new found fans not only support me by buying the book and sharing the experience, but many empathize with our story and can relate to it. Some are happy to share and trust me with their personal experiences by email.

The positive, helpful advice and feedback from the readers and authors in various groups, especially on Facebook, is inspirational. They have helped me add to and enhance my knowledge base, expand my distribution and increase book sales. The act of interacting with my readers is one of the pleasurable aspects of my new career. As I continue to receive emails from readers of 'Glass Half Full', sometimes they quote lines that they liked, enjoyed or can relate to; these lines immediately take me back to that particular moment in time in Australia or the UK. To have had such a profound effect on people through telling our story is more that I could ever have hoped for. I am often asked for my favourite quotes from 'Glass Half Full', these include:

'I cradled Jaime in my arms, rocking her as if she were a baby, until they came with a morphine injection. I could not let anyone else near her. When the injection started to take some effect, alone I gently lifted her onto the bed, where I lay beside her, holding her tightly. I never wanted to let her go again.'

'The women wore too much makeup, for the Queensland sun, heat and humidity. Whilst the men, in their cowboy hats and boots, wear the obligatory wife beater vests. These vests sport food and beer stains and are unattractive even on a well-toned body.'

'However much I tried, my positive spin was in short supply to aid our current situation. We were fortunate; we were alive and well, but life is only worth living when your basic needs are met. Being able to go to our children when they needed us was a basic need, and not a luxury, and this need was not able to be met.'

Another group of people who contact me are writers working on their first manuscript. I still think it odd that they even consider asking me for my advice when I am such a novice and it is obvious to all that I am still learning but I suppose for some it is easier to ask advice from someone who is new to the writing circuit than to approach an established author. I am not proud; I ask anybody for help. My advice for writers considering self-publishing is firstly to join some of the Indie writer/self-published groups and forums. A huge amount of information, knowledge and networking is available that can save you a great deal of time, money and frustration. Secondly, trust your ability as a writer, but use any constructive criticism you receive to enhance your work as self-publisher. Thirdly, keep writing and keep marketing, even on the days when the words do not want to flow or your books appear not to be selling. Keep the faith, because as you will read in many of the networking groups, there are things that happen in the background, even in the quiet times, that will pay dividends when the time is right and not when you want or expect it.

As some of you may know, I have had a tough couple of months due to ill health as this book neared completion. As I continue to overcome some long-term issues, I feel blessed to be able to resume my writing. I am grateful for the messages of support from my newly formed network of author friends, some of whom are now dear friends. Some shared my book links and others wrote posts for social media to share on my behalf. It is reassuring to know that I have made some good friends in a short time.

CHAPTER 20 GYPSY, DREAMER OR BOTH?

As a child growing, up in rural Suffolk, the majority of my upbringing took place with my mum as a single parent with four girls to bring up. In those days, with less available in the form of social security benefits, my mum worked three jobs to ensure that we never went without. Some years we even had a holiday in North Wales in a self-catering caravan. I remember that we moved around a lot, always within Suffolk, but there never appeared to be a particular reason. I think about my childhood a great deal, as a parent myself now. It is natural to want to replicate the positive traits of your parents' style or model of parenting. However, for the same reason, you want to ensure that some traditions and parenting processes stay firmly rooted in the past.

Yesterday, thinking about this in more detail, while working on this, the final chapter of the book, I recalled as a child that Romany gypsies used to come to the door, or stand in the High Street, selling lucky lavender and charms. According to the Oxford English Dictionary the formal definition of the word 'gypsy' is, "a member of a travelling people with dark skin and hair, traditionally living by itinerant trade and fortune telling. Gypsies speak a language (Romany) that is related to Hindi and are believed to have originated in South Asia." While writing the word gypsy in my book, and discussing it with Nigel, I wonder if in today's society, it is politically correct to use the word 'gypsy' or should I say 'travellers' because few are true Romany gypsies now, as a new kind of traveller has evolved. However, when I talk about my childhood, and the Romany gypsies, I remember being mesmerised by their jet-black hair, large gold earrings and the caravans they parked on the playing fields in nearby villages.

My mum always had perfect dyed black hair, which is particularly memorable from my teenage age years when I helped her dye it. I wondered if she was a gypsy or if she had gypsy blood, especially as the informal definition of gypsy is, "a nomadic or free-spirited person."

As strange as it may sound to those who read my books, I never craved travel as a young woman. Admittedly though, I often feel that I am searching for somewhere or something. I always thought my search was for that special somewhere to put down my roots. However, I am discovering that the roots that matter to me are those of my family who are rooted to me. Therefore, if it is a special something that I am searching for, then maybe that something is the true meaning of family. I think my mum was a searcher. Sadly, I do not think she ever found the happiness or contentment she craved or deserved. She was unlucky in love, and in reality made herself a victim by falling for men who would treat her with little respect.

My family is the most important part of my life. As far as finding that special somewhere, that I crave to put down my roots, a piece of my heart belongs to France, but my head will make sure I am always available for my family. The location and lifestyle in France is perfect for me, but there are many challenging aspects of this location. Does that make me a dreamer? This is my first time living in France and there is still so much of France to be explored. How can I know my heart lies here? Is it purely my romantic idealism bolstered by my creative thought processes? Last year when Jaime was hospitalised with her CRPS in the UK and I struggled to get a same day flight to be with her, I first questioned my location choice. Then my estranged daughter Molly made contact with me, to tell me she wanted me back in her life. I struggled with how we could rebuild our relationship after so much time and heartache, especially as she resented me being in France, wanting me to return to the UK. We need to learn from the experiences and challenges that we encounter; otherwise, they are worthless lessons. That is exactly how I feel. No experience, however challenging, is ever wasted time or energy. Life is one lesson we all learn in different ways. My life has seen many giant steps; some would say leaps of learning, some which hurt more than any physical pain. The aching of my heart as if it was being wrenched out haunts me still as I remember losing Molly to Jack, the pain of adultery leading to divorce, and so the list goes on. I am not a materialistic person. Over the years, enduring divorce settlements and relationship break ups, I have lost many precious belongings. However, our humbling experiences in Australia after the floods and now here in France starting over, truly make me appreciate life and all its facets.

As a family, we evaluate the needs of our children and ourselves constantly to ensure that everyone is supported and happy. Who knows where life will take us, but I know that France is home to my heart. I love our little cottage with all its imperfections and idiosyncrasies. I am also aware that as parents, and soon to be grandparents, we have other roles to fulfil for our family, which may cause us to be anywhere in the world, at any given time. Samantha, Cam, and Jaime all yearn to return to Australia over the next few years. Rob is keen to travel especially to Canada, and as I am still searching who knows where I still want or need to go. However, home is where the heart is and my heart belongs to my husband and our wonderful children wherever they or we are in the world.

We arrived in France with just our suitcase and our two Australian cattle dogs. Our French goal or ambition was to undertake one of our many bucket list items. Many aspects of our French experience probably mirror those of other wannabe renovators and expats from the UK, following the dream of a new life in France. We anticipated enjoying the long hot summers. In our new rural setting, we would eat fine food and wine; achieve a more sedate lifestyle, in a country renowned for beautiful architecture and fascinating history. Some of these we manage to do or achieve, whilst some remain on the lengthy 'to do' list. It is important to appreciate that, working on a total renovation whilst living in it, finding the time to explore and enjoy your new country is a challenging pastime. When you add into this scenario learning a new language and dealing with the bureaucracy of setting up your new life, before developing your language skills, you find a recipe for some stressful and testing times.

As a family, with our children currently living in the UK, we enjoyed some amazing highs, combined with some devastating lows this year, as is normal in most families. The lows, as always, are still intensified by the distance from the UK. Although the distance is short, compared to living in Australia, it can seem like thousands of miles away when you physically cannot get there in an emergency.

Another struggle faced this year is one which many UK expats suffer, the inability to find suitable employment in France, regardless of your skills and experience. This is due to not only the level of French language spoken or written, but also the bureaucracy and unemployment rates amongst fluent French speakers. As many do, we had to consider the idea of living apart and one of us commuting to work in the UK. However, in the grand scheme of things, we consider ourselves blessed to have survived for over a year in France without one of us leaving for work. We own a house with no mortgage, albeit a work in progress that we glamp in. We are in reasonably good health, for our age. When I talk about age I speak for myself here being the eldest. Nigel is my toy boy. Anyway, good health enables us to work hard within the constraints of our resources. We achieved one of our bucket list items, buying and starting the renovation of our house in France. We now live nearer to our children, and they have a family home, of sorts, which they can visit and use whenever they want.

We were fortunate to meet some amazing and colourful characters over the last year, French, British and Australian. Some of whom we remain friends with, and some we do not. As in any country, you do not always find things in common with everyone just because you are the same nationality. Some people expect that to be the case here, but for us it certainly is not. We love the sense of community here, especially amongst the French. Their generosity of spirit and knowledge is something I have never experienced before in the UK or Australia. As the renovation continues, and I near completion of this my second book, which picks up our story as we arrive in France, it looks like another busy year ahead for us. With so many happy memories already made we a great deal to look forward to as we, continue our new life in Charente.

There are many funny little incidents involving our French neighbours since our arrival, some of which are in the previous chapters. However, it only fitting to end with one that relates to our beloved neighbour Andre. This elderly French man accepted us at face value. Unable to understand a word I said whilst trying to get to know each other, he has laughed at me, hugged me and wiped the mud from my face. He protected us from eating poisonous mushrooms and fed us with his marrows, beetroot, tomatoes and green beans in desperate times, even though he did not know they were desperate for us. We have seen, spoken to, or waved to Andre almost every day since September 2012. On days when we do not see him or his wife we are immediately concerned. However, we need not be, he is a hardy man. He rubs his back and pretends to cry after a hard day digging. Sometimes he rubs his shoulder after cutting trees with his chainsaw for hours on end. Despite this, he is likely to be living and working his land for many years to come. I envy the strength, stamina and work ethic of these elderly French people who now are my neighbours. I dread the day when something happens to one of them. I hope it is not a house of cards that will crumble when one of the pieces of this tight knit community is removed. They are like one big family. They walk in and out of each other's houses, never lock their doors and freely pick weeds from each other's gardens and plant pots whilst chatting.

Even though we value their friendship sometimes when you are having a down day, the thought of these mentally taxing conversations when we are out walking the boys is too much to bear. On previous occasions like this, we walk a different route, or at a slower or faster pace to get away with just a salutary wave from a distance. On one such occasion when Nigel had had no work for a week and we were debating our monetary situation whilst walking, we saw Andre in his garden in the distance.

"Oh no, I can't do this, not now." Nigel says.

"It's okay; you walk on ahead I will speak to him." As we near the bridge into the village, Andre is standing near the entrance to Yvette's driveway, which runs behind his outside kitchen.

"He's taking a leak." Nigel says.

"Don't be silly, he's not doing that in the rain."

Nigel looks at me in that way he does, again. It is a common site in France to see men at the side of the road relieving their full bladders with no apparent concern for passers-by. We even went to a vide grenier one Sunday, and the parking attendant was relieving himself at the entrance with a tomato sandwich in his free hand. As we get nearer, I can see that Nigel is right. Now the problem intensifies not only do we need to pass without chatting but also we need to pass without the daily welcoming handshake. Fortunately, the rain suddenly lashes down as Andre makes his way across the road waving as he catches a glimpse of us before closing the front door. That was a lucky escape. After sixteen months in France from a renovation viewpoint, the house has evolved and is emerging like a phoenix from the ashes. From a work and financial perspective, we are surviving. My writing career is progressing steadily, book sales and interest in my other writing projects increases week on week. As our family continues to grow, some of the children are spreading their wings as education, adulthood, and opportunity leads them to pastures new. Are we settled? Is this it? The seeds we planted here germinated, but are the roots strong enough to hold my gypsy blood and us in place? On the other hand, will my nomadic free spirit move us on to another country or another big adventure? Watch this space.

My parting piece of advice for anyone visiting France is; beware of the welcoming gesture of a handshake from a French man. You never know, he may have recently responded to the call of nature and his urine sprinkled hand could be touching yours any moment!

ABOUT THE AUTHOR

Author Sarah Jane Butfield was born in Ipswich and raised in rural Suffolk, England.

Fulfilling her childhood dream and becoming a nurse, was just the start of her amazing journey. Her nursing and teaching qualifications would take her around the world, enabling her to work in all fields of nursing, education and management. However, after 27 years as nurse, wife and mother of four children and three step-children, Sarah Jane has now achieved another long held ambition, that of becoming a published author.

'Glass Half Full: Our Australian Adventure', her debut travel memoir, has been followed by this sequel, 'Two Dogs and a Suitcase: Clueless in Charente'. The expat kitchen garden journal – 'Our Frugal Summer in Charente', to accompany the sequel, is due for release later this year. In addition to her non-fiction books, she is also a published freelance magazine journalist and blogger, in the healthcare and writing arenas. Sarah Jane is currently working on a series of self-help books for people facing challenging life events and tough family situations, based on her real life experience of divorce, bereavement, child custody issues, migration, parenting, etc.

Thank you for reading.

NOTE FROM THE AUTHOR:

Reviews are gold to authors! If you have enjoyed this book, would you consider rating it and reviewing it on the site where you purchased your copy?

Chat with me and other memoir authors and readers in our Facebook group, We Love Memoirs:
https://www.facebook.com/groups/welovememoirs/

You'll get a warm welcome!

If you would like news of new releases, previews and special offers for fans, subscribe to my personal mailing list, Sarah Jane's Memoirs. There will be no spam emails, I promise. http://eepurl.com/0IuML

TRAVEL MEMOIRS
by
Sarah Jane Butfield

Sarah Jane's travel memoirs are available at online bookstores worldwide, all links are available on her author website at http://sarahjanebutfield.wix.com/sarahjanebutfield

Glass Half Full: Our Australian Adventure

Is the glass half-empty or half full? Ironically, sometimes life influences our view and alters our perception.

When a UK step-family makes the tough decision to seek a new life in Australia it appears all their troubles are over as their new life begins. Life in Australia exceeds their expectations until challenging life events including grief, loss and relationship issues test their powers of positivity, persistence and determination. However, a bigger test was coming. When they lose their home, assets and belongings to the Brisbane floods in January 2011 they have to decide when enough is enough! A touching true story that many readers will relate to.

Two dogs and a suitcase: Clueless in Charente

The title says it all: what we have and where we are. This book, the sequel to Glass Half Full: Our Australian Adventure, follows our French exploits as we endeavour to rebuild our lives in another new country, after spending four and half years in Australia. Our goal, or hope for the immediate future, is to focus positively on the present, so that we can start a new, optimistic future back in Europe. Our main aim is to be nearer to the children, leaving the dark clouds of the challenges we faced in Australia as a distant memory. Journey with us as we arrive in rural South West France; enjoy my reflections, thoughts, and observations about my family, our new surroundings, and our lifestyle. Follow the journey of my writing career and how we start our renovation project while managing our convoluted family life. Once again, we will laugh, cry, and enjoy life to the fullest with a generous helping of positive spin thrown in for good measure.

Our Frugal Summer in Charente

Voted one of the top 50 self-published books worth reading 2015`!

Meet Sarah Jane, a woman with a reputation for culinary catastrophe who tries to keep her family fed in challenging circumstances in rural France. Frugal living was not part of the plan when they arrived from Australia to undertake the renovation of a quaint cottage in the Charente. However, when life throws them a curve-ball the challenge was set. How to survive in France with very little money and two Australian cattle dogs. The answer came in the form of 5 chickens, 4 ducks and a vegetable garden! The frugal plan was to save money by any means possible, to enable any money they could earn to be invested into continuing the renovation of the cottage. In true 'Good Life' style Sarah Jane attacks this challenge head on by keeping some small livestock and converting a garden, that resembled a meadow, into a French 'potager' or kitchen garden. The French tradition of using produce from their 'potagers' is renowned for enabling families to create meals that are healthy, cost effective and simple. There are 31 recipes for a variety of food and drinks, included in a month by month account, of how they transformed a neglected garden into a frugal yet productive expat kitchen garden.

Photobooks to accompany the travel memoir series
Book 1 Views Through My Lens: Hobart and surrounding areas.
Permanently free at all bookstores
http://sarahjanebutfield.wix.com/sarahjanebutfield

Taking up photography, as a cathartic exercise, after losing almost everything to the Brisbane floods in 2011 gave Nigel a different perspective on life and his Australian surroundings. There is an old saying that a person's eyes are the "window to their soul." We have found that our photographs are the window to our memories. This is the first book in a series from places we have lived, visited and enjoyed which we hope will appeal not only to followers of our adventures, but also to people who are interested in photography or travel.

Photobook 2 due for release later this year.

OTHER BOOKS BY SARAH JANE BUTFIELD

The Nomadic Nurse Series
Book 1 Ooh Matron!

Sarah Jane has no career aspirations, all she wants is to leave school, work as a cashier at Woolworths and get married. Then everything changes and she finds herself wearing a fluorescent pink uniform and studying to get into Nursing School. What inspired this surprising change of direction? What happens when she leaves home to live in a garrison town with a housemate who is a party animal? The big question being, is she really cut out to be a nurse?

Let's start at the beginning with Sarah Jane as a sixteen-year-old country girl, a bit old fashioned but who has a mischievous sense of humour and who suddenly decides she wants to be a nurse!

"This funny, yet poignant nursing memoir has Sarah Jane's trademark honest writing style which shines through in every story she tells. From starting her student nurse training in Essex to coping with patients in happy, sad and heart-breaking situations. It gives you a young woman's view into the realities of entering the world of nursing in the 1980's. A highly entertaining and informative memoir which was able to take me from laughing out loud to having welled tears of empathy." S. Brewster

EPILOGUE

My faith has also been extremely important to me during this year and in particularly the following bible quotes:

Proverbs 3: 5, 6

"Trust in the Lord with all your heart, and lean not on your own understanding. In all your ways acknowledge him, and he will make your paths straight."

James 1: 5-6

"If any of you lacks wisdom, he should ask God, who gives generously to all without finding fault, and it will be given to him. But when he asks he must believe and not doubt because he who doubts is like a wave of the sea, blown and tossed by the wind."

I hope that my books 'Glass Half Full: Our Australian Adventure' and 'Two Dogs and a Suitcase: Clueless in Charente', will inspire and motivate people who are facing challenging life events. To give just one person a sense of hope, that there is always a way out, an answer, would be amazing. If you can view your glass as half full even in the toughest times, you have the best chance of moving forward. Believe in dreaming big, working hard to ensure success and having fun.

In life as we move forward with our personal dreams and ambitions, our daily mantra remains:

You have to Conceive it, and Believe it, to ensure you Achieve it.

It is posted to our dream board as our daily inspiration. As we tick off our achievements, the words gain momentum. Make this your mantra for achieving your dreams.

PROFESSIONAL ACKNOWLEDGEMENTS

Darren Pitts: English Estate Agent in France.

Website: http://www.immojr.com/

Tim Day: Sky Builders. Le Grange, Champoury, Edon. 16320

CONTACT SARAH JANE BUTFIELD

Email: sjbutfield@gmail.com

https://www.facebook.com/AuthorSarahJaneButfield

http://sarahjanebutfield-glass-half-full.blogspot.co.uk/

https://twitter.com/SarahJanewrites

Follow @SarahJanewrites

http://sarahjanebutfield.wix.com/sarahjanebutfield

Printed in Great Britain
by Amazon